THE BELL RINGS AT FOUR

Well I think Mrs. Dorothy R. Robinson is about the best woman there is. She is also a great teacher, if I do say so myself. She works very hard. She has two jobs and she is very good at both. I love her very much. The End.

THE BELL RINGS AT FOUR

AT FOUR *A Black*

Teacher's Chronicle of Change

by

DOROTHY REDUS ROBINSON

MADRONA PRESS · AUSTIN, TEXAS

ISBN 0-89052-024-0
Library of Congress Catalog Card No. 78-61472
Copyright 1978 by Dorothy Redus Robinson. All rights reserved

FIRST EDITION

Manufactured in the United States of America

MADRONA PRESS, INC.
Box 3750
Austin, Texas 78764

Frontispiece: Note written in 1974 by second-grade-student Tracy Sumrall

*To my brother George who taught me to read;
my parents who encouraged reading; my husband
who shared my love for reading; and all of the
boys and girls whom I taught to read.*

CONTENTS

ILLUSTRATIONS

Picture sections following pages 50 and 98

FOREWORD

Bowed by the weight of centuries
He leans upon His hoe and gazes
on the ground. The emptiness of
ages on his face, and on his back
the burden of the world.
                    —EDWIN MARKHAM

I remember not being able to wait until I reached the fifth grade—Mrs. Denson's room. Mrs. Denson rang the bell for the Booker T. Washington Elementary School in Marlin, Texas. She often let privileged students ring it, and I recall the thrill I got the first time I rang it for the end of the noon recess.

Many teachers look at their profession as "the burden of the world." Dorothy Robinson says, "I was privileged to ring the bell." Over four decades in the classroom settling disputes, chairing projects, wiping tears, cleaning wounds, running errands—teaching—and Dorothy Robinson says it was a privilege!

Ancestral History—Big Meeting. These are terms found in the story of a young black woman's life in South and later East Texas. In the first chapter of her book, Mrs Robinson explains, "I learned much of my ancestral history by reading gravestones as I helped players search for balls lost in the far reaches of the cemetery when a proud batter 'knocked a home run.'"

In a later chapter she defines a still-practiced East Texas tradition—the "Big Meeting." I particularly like her definition. The

Big Meeting was " . . . a homecoming, a fashion show, a food fair, a lovers' paradise, and an exhibition of religious emotionalism." Her language is picturesque and quotable. When she describes a disappointment, she says it was "a weird mixture of gut bitterness, smouldering anger, and helpless surrender."

However, there is a rather small phrase that gripped my imagination like no other in the book. Mrs. Robinson relates her initiation into special education. She explains her negative reaction on first viewing retarded children. Her mentor advised, "Go back and see a child. . . . " Dorothy Robinson has helped to erase the "emptiness of ages" from the faces of many a near-forgotten child. She has done her share to lift the burdens. I sincerely hope you enjoy reading this book. I hope it inspires you to put something of your life on paper so that those who were not around when it happened will have a legacy on which to build.

I am grateful to Mrs. Robinson for writing this book. It is a book that should have been written. She reminds us of the struggle of black education in Texas in the early years. She tells her story without bitterness, without blame. She simply tells it like it happened. She tells her story with humor, sadness, joy, and the other realities that come with life. She makes no apologies. It is a well-written book. If anything, Mrs. Robinson treats her villains too graciously. But then that's Dorothy Robinson. She was privileged to ring the bell—I am privileged to know the bell ringer.

John Hill Westbrook, *Pastor*
True Vine Baptist Church

Tyler, Texas
August 1, 1978

THE BELL RINGS AT FOUR

A TEACHER IN THE FAMILY

*P*APA STOOD ON THE sidewalk in front of a restaurant in the Negro section of town. Today it would be referred to as the black neighborhood. The date was October 1, 1928, the town was Cuero, Texas, and papa was Caleb Redus. He stood tall and prideful, dressed in his excellently laundered khaki suit which mama had ironed using a pallet on the floor as an ironing board.

In all of my growing-up years, I never knew mama to use a regular ironing board. She would place an old quilt on the floor, cover it with a sheet, and sit with one foot folded under her, a sort of Oriental fashion, cuddling a whimpering toddler within the triangle of her legs, and do the family ironing while softly humming a hymn. The khaki suit that papa wore on this crisp October morning was ample testimony of her skill in this operation.

I was dressed in the tan crash suit that my roommate had made in the Home Economics Department at Prairie View College. The material had cost twenty-five cents a yard. My new tan and brown shoes, which matched the suit perfectly, had been ordered from the National Cloak and Suit Company and had cost $2.98.

I was proud of papa and he was proud of me. I stood with him, poignantly aware of my importance. Hadn't I spent a whole year at Prairie View College? Did I not have tucked away in my trunk at this very minute a statement from S.M.S. Marrs, the state superintendent, declaring that I was eligible for a temporary certificate of three years' duration; and that in due time, I would receive the

revered document so it could be registered in the office of the county superintendent, thus making me a full-fledged teacher eligible
to receive pay for services rendered? This fact was paramount in
both our minds, but it was papa who dared costume our mental
concentrations with words. To a friend he said with ill-concealed
pride, "Dorothy is going to take up her work on Monday." By that
he meant that I would begin my first year of teaching.

It did mean that, but it meant even more to papa. It represented
what the psychologists of the day termed "parental projection."
For him, it probably meant also a form of revenge—a personal satisfaction derived from triumph over opposing philosophies of land-
lords, associates, and even some relatives. As Caleb Redus stood
there in this agricultural South Texas town seeing his eldest daughter off to "take up her work," he surely saw in her a realization of
his own vanquished youthful dreams. He recalled anew the hurt
and despair that he had known some thirty years earlier, when he
was forced to decline a scholarship to Paul Quinn College in Waco,
Texas, because there was no one at home to help his widowed "ma"
pay the mortgage on their seventy-two acre farm.

Papa's was a keen creative mind, and he had a thorough and objective evaluation of himself. A famous educator once said in one
of my classes, "If a child is bright enough to be called bright, he is
bright enough to know that he is bright." Papa was no child, but
he was bright and he knew it. So he probably experienced greater
emotional suffering because of his lack of formal education than a
person of lesser intelligence would have.

Recalling the barriers he had encountered in his efforts to send
his children to school, he could not have failed to remember that
some four years earlier, a few blocks away from where he stood,
the county superintendent had told him, "Caleb, niggers don't need
any education." This was in response to papa's request to transfer
his two oldest children into a district that provided a high school
for Negro children when no such institution existed in his own
home district.

Also at this moment, his mind no doubt housed the memory of
the numerous times his landlord suggested, "You take those kids
out of school and have them help gather this crop." Sometimes the

same idea garnered the strong support of papa's childless brothers. A sharecropper though he was, he turned a stone-deaf ear to all such suggestions.

School would begin on Monday, October 3, but the independence of my professional life was born on this particular morning when papa placed the train ticket in my hand at the San Antonio and Aransas Pass depot, told me that my trunk was checked to Hallettsville, Texas, and assured me that Uncle Benja and Aunt Baby would surely meet me there. To say goodbye, we shook hands. To have kissed in public would have embarrassed papa.

On the train I gave some thought as to how I would approach my work. Yes, I had had a year's study at Prairie View College, and my courses had included psychology; but as I recall now, I, in planning my year's work, relied more on what I had seen my elementary teachers do than on what I had learned at Prairie View. This in no way indicates the quality of instruction at Prairie View; rather, it bespeaks my lack of background to accept meaningfully the offerings of the college.

This recall of what I had seen my own elementary teachers do was not all bad for, by remembering their improvisations, substitutions, and ingenuity, I provided myself with a sort of built-in ability to cope with the complete lack of aids, materials, equipment, and supervision that even then were considered basic. I knew what I would find along this line come Monday morning—*nothing*—and that is exactly what I found.

Uncle Benja and Aunt Baby did meet me in Hallettsville. My trunk was claimed amid repeated embraces. There was no embarrassment here with this young couple. Wasn't I Uncle Benja's sister's child; and wasn't Aunt Baby my blood cousin, being the daughter of papa's sister? Furthermore, I was the first teacher from either side of the family. I was a precious symbol. Through me the families were pushing their boundaries farther from the field work and domestic chores, which to my parent's generation still held deep connotations of slavery.

In Uncle Benja's 1925 Ford—which had to be cranked manually— we drove the twelve miles to their farm home in the Wellersburg community where I was to teach. I was to live with Uncle Benja

and Aunt Baby without paying any room or board. This was a blessing of inconceivable magnitude, since my salary was to be $52.50
per month for the school term of four and one-half months. Years
later, a superintendent in Anderson County, Texas, was to tell me
that no teacher had ever taught for such a short term and for such
a low salary. My reply to him was that many black teachers of that
period worked under such circumstances. Incidentally, that one-
half month proved to be of tremendous importance years later
when my retirement benefits were being computed. Because of it
the 1928-29 school year was accepted as a legal school year.

The farm belonging to Uncle Benja and Aunt Baby Aycock was
located about half a mile from the one-room schoolhouse that had
been built around the turn of the century with funds collected by
local blacks among themselves and dedicated to "school and church
purposes." This building was on the site of the log structure in
which both papa and mama had attended school in the late 1880s
and 1890s.

Lacking both in architectural beauty and utilitarian aspects, the
small building, about twenty by thirty feet, stood in stark ugliness
in one corner of a cemetery bordered on two sides by dark, thick
woods. The absence of evergreens, and the cold grayness of the
long blankets of Spanish moss gave these woods a ghostly appearance. The schoolhouse had never been touched by a paint brush.
The wooden walls had never been planed. To touch the surface
with the hand or any other part of the body was to risk picking up
a painful splinter. The seats—there were no desks—were long enough
to accommodate five or six pupils and were built of the same rough
lumber used for the walls. Continued use by restless bottoms had
proved to be an effective planing device, and the danger of splinters
was reduced to near zero. Four small windows were the only source
of light.

In the back of the single-room building was a raised platform and
a crude lectern, which itinerant ministers used as their pulpit. The
school children used a shelf in this structure to store their lunch
pails. Young persons today would find it difficult indeed to visual-
ize the beauty that it is possible to achieve through the artistic arrangement of Karo syrup buckets and Rex apple jelly buckets.

There was no playground equipment, no plantings to enhance the landscape, and only one ramshackle outdoor surface toilet. There was not even a source of water supply. There was a rusty wood-burning heater but no wood.

As doleful and discouraging as the picture was, it did not faze me, for I had not been accustomed to very much more. Actually, our immediate and urgent needs were met when parents responded to my call and took turns bringing loads of firewood, and the children took turns bringing drinking water from home.

My enrollment totaled nineteen. Few of my charges referred to me as "Miss Redus." "Cousin Dorithy" (long *i*) was the more frequent title. Indeed, I was related to many of them, as I had been born in this community and both of my parents had grown up there. Attendance was excellent. Only extreme weather or an occasional bout with a minor illness resulted in absences. In this group of pupils, there were absolutely no disciplinary problems, although one student was only two years younger than I, and there were none who gave evidence of being emotionally disturbed.

Perhaps one or two were mentally retarded, and certainly there were two or three slow learners, but since the practice of tagging children with educational labels had not then gained strong foothold and sanction, the youngsters did not know that they were different and I did not think of them as presenting special problems. With available textbooks, pictures, discarded magazines, nuts, sticks, grains of corn, and creative games, the children were taught, and hopefully, each learned what he was capable of learning.

With homemade string balls and bats cut from near-by woods and trimmed to fit hands of various sizes, the game of baseball was as popular in January as it usually is in July. I learned much of my ancestral history by reading gravestones as I helped players search for balls lost in the far reaches of the cemetery when a proud batter "knocked a home run."

At the end of each twenty-day teaching period, Uncle Benja accompanied me to the home of each of the three trustees to receive his signature on my voucher. This was usually on Friday afternoon. The following day I would accompany Uncle Benja and Aunt Baby to Hallettsville, where the superintendent would approve my check and I would cash it. I do not recall being especially proud or excited about my earnings. Reading matter constituted my chief purchases.

Perhaps the youngsters whom I taught this first year were without ambition, or perhaps I failed to provide motivation, for none ever became great leaders or gained renown for excellence in any field of endeavor, but to the best of my knowledge none ever developed criminal records. They became honest, hard-working citizens. Most of them are still engaged in farming and ranching.

So for four and one-half months I was so busy I scarcely realized the passage of time. I walked the half mile to school, my route taking me across a pasture stocked with Hereford cows. Although farm reared, I was desperately afraid of the white-faced bull that seemed to have a regular schedule of breakfasting so close to my path I could smell his breath. Uncle Benja reminded me daily, and quite truthfully, that the bull was as tame as a house cat, but his assurance did little to calm my fears.

My busy schedule also included collecting broomweed and mare's-tail, which I used each morning to start the fire in the heater so the room would be warm when the children arrived. My mother had informed me of the superb value of these dry weeds as kindling.

I kept busy also trying to plan and supervise Halloween, Thanksgiving, and Christmas parties at the school to bring some amusement into the quiet and dull lives of both the young people and the adults of the community; sending notes to parents whose turn it was to supply firewood; gathering wild pecans and hickory nuts during weekends; and walking the mile to the rural mailbox for the weekly letter from Frank, who later became my husband.

So my first year of teaching ended. I am not sure that any formal instrument for measuring achievement would have yielded a plus had it been applied to my pupils, but I do know that I had achieved. I had gained a new knowledge about myself, and knew now that I could fill a teaching post. I knew that I related well to both children and their parents; that I could cope with deficiencies; and most fundamental of all, I knew that I liked teaching and that I wanted to make it my life's career. Yet when the trustees asked me if I wanted to contract with the school to teach for another year, I simply said, "No, the job does not pay enough." Oh, my profound innocence and naiveté! I did not know the impact of the depression, which even then was a specter on the economic horizon.

The fact that my school term was short was a blessing in one respect. It enabled me to return to Prairie View for the third quarter, which began in early March.

For the most part, the $236.25 that represented the total of my first year's earnings, was spent as it was collected. Monthly I sent money to my oldest brother who was attending Prairie View. I had assembled a meager personal wardrobe suitable for both the spring quarter and the summer session, which I also planned to attend. I had given Uncle Benja $7.50 to help pay his taxes and I had, of course, bought Christmas presents for papa, mama, and other members of the family.

So upon the closing of school, I borrowed some ninety dollars from the First State Bank in Yoakum, Texas, to help finance my second venture at Prairie View. With the help of my high school principal, money had been borrowed from this bank to help finance my schooling at Prairie View the year before. With the help of this second loan, early in 1929, I again became a coed.

AWAY FROM
MY FATHER'S HOUSE

$\mathcal{B}$Y THE END of July I had begun to recognize the gravity of my error in not accepting a contract to teach the Wellersberg school a second year. Throughout the summer session I had inquired about vacancies across the state, and had written numerous applications, many of which were never honored with a reply. The responses received were discouragingly negative. Instead of filling vacancies, many school officials were concerned with staff reductions and salary cuts.

My spirit was far from buoyant when summer school closed and I went home. Home now was a new location, as my parents had moved to Bay City, Texas.

Poor papa! In those years he still had dreams of finding his treasure in a bumper cotton crop. So he had rented a farm—or rather a part of a large plantation—on the banks of the Colorado River in Matagorda County. Here the soil was better suited to the growing of cotton than it was in the Cuero area. His crop that year was indeed a bountiful one, but the price was a strong indicator of the seriousness of the depression that was upon us.

I arrived at the farm at the beginning of the cotton picking season and, having been well indoctrinated by both parents that all honest labor was honorable, I entertained neither reluctance nor embarrassment in "giving a hand." My responsibility was to record the weights and keep separate accounts of each of the cotton pickers. This was a considerable chore as, at the height of the harvest season, more than one bale of cotton was picked daily. This meant that there was almost always someone at the scales to have his bag of cotton weighed and checked and the amount recorded.

To check a sack of cotton it was necessary to examine it for burs, leaves, and even sand. A dishonest or careless picker could increase the weight of his load and reduce the ultimate value of the cotton by including such superfluous materials in his sack. Indeed a few pickers were not averse to throwing in an occasional handful of soil. A picker who resorted to such a dastardly practice when harvesting for Caleb Redus was apt to find himself in painful and embarrassing circumstances. In 1929, before the era of the mechanical cotton picker, the production of a bale of cotton was a source of pride and papa's regard for "clean cotton" approached fetishism. This feeling led him to develop the ability to grade cotton with remarkable success. Frequently before taking a bale to the gin, he would forecast its classification and upon his return he would relate with pride, "I hit the nail on the head."

Sometimes when I had a respite from the scales and the bookkeeping, I put on a sack and picked cotton too. Papa paid me for my work. That was not unusual and in no way indicated that he felt my adult status obligated him to pay me, for he always paid his children for work done at harvest time. Our pay scale was usually one-half that of the regular hired help. With mama's guidance, we used our money to purchase clothing and school supplies. Any remaining funds were lent to papa, and he paid us interest or invested the money for us in a cow or a pig.

It was in this field setting, on an early October day, that I saw a small black Ford coupe stop at the end of the cotton rows. The Reverend S.M. Dedman, whom I had known since early childhood, stepped out. When he was close enough to be understood, he said in his booming voice, "Girl, don't you have a teaching certificate? Put down that sack and come with me; I have a job for you." In the years since, I have heard great symphonies performed by renowned artists in the grand music halls of this and other continents; I have heard poetic renditions by great readers; I have heard the shrill warble of the mockingbird and the robin's spring song; but to this day I still feel that the words of the Reverend Mr. Dedman brought the most welcome sound my ears have ever heard.

Perhaps this incident holds special meaning for me because it represents one of my early experiences with prayer, and prayer has been, and still is, a vital force in my life. Anyway, I had prayed daily for a teaching job and here, according to this old minister, was the answer to my prayers.

While mama fried an extra chicken—for certainly the minister had dinner with us—I prepared to present myself as an applicant for the teaching position in the Markham Colored School in Markham, Texas.

In papa's old Ford, he and I followed Mr. Dedman the twenty-odd miles to Markham, stopping finally at the home of a missionary sister who led us to the proper school official. This trustee served the school board as personnel director, and as everything else, as I was to learn later. It was he who would either hire me or reject my application. Before leaving her home, the missionary lady told us why the school was without a teacher on what was to have been the opening day.

A young woman who held the bachelor's degree from Prairie View College had contracted for the school but had failed to report for duty. There was no official word from her, but it was being whispered in the community that she had accepted a position in Corpus Christi.

With this information, the four of us presented ourselves to the trustee who, incidentally, was owner and operator of the main store of that village of some 400 persons. His was a smalltown department store stocking groceries, dry goods, drugs, hardware, and notions. He was a pleasant man of unhurried movements and, while interviewing a prospective teacher was not distasteful, it was not of sufficient importance to warrant his real concern. His one question, as I recall, was to inquire if I had a teaching certificate. Then he told me that if the teacher who had contracted for the position did not appear by noon the following day the school was mine.

It was then that I changed the words of my daily prayer. I no longer asked God for a job; rather, I prayed that the teacher who was under contract would not appear. The following day about noon papa and I again appeared at Mr. Barber's store and were told that the other teacher had not honored the contract, so the job was mine. He gave me a zinc water bucket, a dipper, and a box of chalk and said, "We'll get you some wood down there before the first norther comes." While I have never heard these exact words repeated by a school official, they are significant because that quick transaction was typical of the measures used to provide the needs of the Negro schools of that day and for many years afterward. Indeed, this approach had not completely disappeared as late as the mid-1960s.

Materials, supplies, and equipment for Negro schools were inadequate or nonexistent, the lack justified by declaring insufficient funds. The belief was held by many, and expressed by some, that money spent on the education of Negroes was a waste, or that educated Negroes "got out of their places" and proved to be bad influences among others.

Facility-wise, the Markham school did not differ greatly from the Wellersberg school. It too, was a one-room affair, but it had six windows and two doors and had once received a coat of white paint. This paint had long since yielded to the ravages of the coastal area's salt air and, with the attitude about education for Negroes and the tight money situation of the depression, I don't suppose anyone ever gave any thought to a new paint job. I know I did not. Here too, the campus was bare with no plantings and no playground equipment. Unlike the Wellersberg school, the Markham school boasted two surface toilets. There was a hand pump that usually had to be primed before any water poured forth. Sometimes even the priming was fruitless, and water had to be carried from a nearby private well. There was no storage facility of any kind. A small, rickety table served as the teacher's desk. Pupils' desks were commercial products with metal supports of intricate design resembling the fretwork of the New Orleans French Quarter. Even when new, this furniture probably was more beautiful than practical. Anyway, by the time I inherited the desks, they already had seen years of use in the white school (I was told). Ink stains, carved initials, missing nuts and bolts, and a general dilapidated condition gave strong testimony of long prior use somewhere.

Some of the desks were absolutely beyond use and, in interest of physical safety, I relegated several to the only storage place I could find—an area underneath the building, which was accessible because there was no underpinning. I kept enough to accommodate my thirty-odd pupils, but there was little I could do to enhance their adequacy. Frequently the order of my classroom was disrupted when the slight movement of a small body brought desk and occupant down in a heap of rusty metal, splintered wood, and howling humanity.

Like the desks, the textbooks bespoke prior use and abuse. While the number of books was sufficient, missing sections and torn pages presented problems.

Here the similarities of the Markham school and the Wellersberg school ended. The communities differed in population, economy, and social aspirations. Wellersberg was a farming community with each family owning its farm and maintaining itself as a stable social unit. Markham was an agricultural community too, and the people earned their livelihood through agricultural pursuits, but the Negro families did not own the farms. They worked as laborers, returning at the end of the day to their homes "in town." Most of these homes were two- or three-room shacks. Family life was fragmented. Most of the children were from broken homes and were being reared by grandparents or by the mother alone. The men of the community found their chief employment in the rice and cotton fields. Once these crops were harvested, they spent many idle hours walking the streets or playing dominoes around a wood heater in some overcrowded dwelling.

Some of the women picked cotton, but they found more permanent employment as domestic workers. In many families, especially during the winter months, the mother's wages from domestic chores constituted the total income. A cook who earned $3.50 per week was fortunate, as was a washerwoman who received 75 cents for doing the week's laundry for a family of five. This entailed arduous physical labor, for automatic washers had not yet come into general use.

Low wages, naturally, were reflected in teachers' salaries. I had refused to renew my contract at Wellersberg because the pay was too low, but I was exuberantly happy to accept work at Markham for fifty dollars per month. The school term, however, was of six months duration instead of four, and that was a redeeming feature. The terms of my contract were never specified in writing. In fact, I do not think I ever signed a contract during my entire four-year tenure at Markham. I was fortunate to find living quarters with a widow and her six-year-old granddaughter. Mrs. Roberta Turner was one of the most unforgettable characters I have ever known. Her husband had died quite young, leaving her with one daughter, whom she had reared. Now she was rearing her granddaughter. She was tough, yet tender; wise, yet humble; lacking in formal education, but inspired in soul and mind. We became very close friends. To me she was a mother figure, a social counselor, and a professional adviser. Her granddaughter now is the widow of the late Dr. J. A. Phillips of Minden, Louisiana, and, as Mrs. Ellen Phillips, holds a responsible position with the Houston public schools. She is one of several of my former students who participated in a testimonial program on my retirement from teaching in May, 1974.

I paid Mrs. Turner $1.00 per week for room rent. I boarded myself and budgeted $1.50 per week for groceries. It is inconceivable now to recall that one could prepare twenty-one nutritious, palatable meals at such a small cost. Vegetables and meat brought from home on my weekend visits helped to stretch my food budget.

As fall weather changed to winter, my trips home became less frequent. Such trips were hazardous, for even a light rain could make the roads impassable. The paved highways now common were the exception then. I was determined to make a success of my work in Markham, and I felt that missing a day at school for any reason besides illness would be a mark against me.

Since the Markham school was in an independent school district, it was not necessary for the county superintendent to approve my voucher. My checks, like those of the white teachers, were signed at the school board meetings. At the end of the pay period, I had only to go by Mr. Barber's store and pick it up. On one or two occasions, the trustees forgot to sign my check. I have never ceased to wonder how such an oversight could have occurred and if the signing of the other teachers' checks was forgotten also.

Anyway, on the weekend that I received my paycheck, I usually

trusted God and the elements and went home, in spite of travel dif-
ficulties. Sometimes my parents came for me. Otherwise, I went
by train, the *B and M* (Brownsville and Mexico) to Bay City, where
I was met.

My meager salary was willingly shared with other family members. My oldest brother was in his second year at Prairie View. A
sister was in junior high school in Bay City, and money was needed
for her room and board. I contributed monthly to the needs of
these two and still had a dollar or two to pass on to papa in an
emergency.

I am not sure that my teaching technique improved during my
second year. Certainly there was little in the school environment
to encourage advancement in any area. The sheer joy of teaching
combined with youthful energy motivated me to do my best each
day. But there was more; there was a sort of mystical aura about
my work at Markham. There I was not "Cousin Dorithy"; I was
"Miss Redus," and I was accorded the special deference with which
public school teachers of that day were generally regarded. The
people of the community expected much of me and demanded with
a friendly eagerness that their expectations be fulfilled. I was asked
to teach Sunday school, write orders to Sears and Roebuck, write
letters, and figure up weekly wages.

It never occurred to me to refuse their varied requests. In fact,
I rather enjoyed this kind of personal contact and the comfortable
relationship that developed between me and the people of the community. I became not merely the childrens' teacher but also the
community's, and everyone referred to me as "our teacher."

To this day I feel that the layman's use of the term, *our teacher*,
is a more valid measurement of teacher effectiveness than many of
the formal evaulative criteria used.

Another factor that helped in the development and maintenance
of the community's high regard for me was my almost complete
lack of social life. Today this would be considered an unwhole-
some situation. After all, I was only twenty years old. But in 1929
there were still some vestiges of the idea that teaching was an old
maid's profession, and to disassociate oneself from the opposite sex

was a sort of saintly virtue. It was not generally known that I was engaged to Frank James Robinson but, even so, there were no likely choices among the young men of the community.

Just as the economy and social structure of Markham differed from that of Wellersberg, so did my students. I do not believe that there was more innate ability among the Markham children, but there was definitely more expressed ambition and more overt aggression, both positive and negative. Some of these youngsters later became distinguished in education, business, and health-service fields. One boy, whom I was always inclined to regard as a manifest troublemaker, and whose behavior I was never able to modify noticeably, served a term in the Texas State Penitentiary. I never knew the nature of his offense. I do not claim credit for the success of some of these former students, nor do I assume responsibility for the failure of others; but, in fairness to all, I suppose I contributed in some measure to both.

Little was said and less was done about the limited budget the school officials allocated for the operation of the Negro school. This is not to say that there was not a general awareness of the inequity. Somehow I learned what the state per-capita appropriation was for that school year. I do not recall the exact amount, but I multiplied the per-capita figure by the number of children I had enrolled. The result confirmed what I already knew. There was a grave disparity between the state allocation and the actual expenditures. Absolutely nothing was spent on that school during the year except the $300 for my salary and the insignificant cost of two or three cords of wood, and two or three boxes of chalk.

One day I mentioned this to the trustee with whom I did all of my official transactions. He turned a violent red and retorted very sternly, "Dorothy, are you accusing someone of misappropriation of funds? That is a serious accusation." I replied, perhaps not with equal sternness, "I am accusing no one of anything. I am simply saying that the money is not being received by the school where I work." The matter was pursued no further, but the following year, I received a five-dollar-a-month raise, a matter of particular significance when salaries were being slashed and work forces reduced throughout the nation.

Early in the school year, I called a meeting of all citizens, and we organized a Parent-Teacher Association (PTA). This organization became a vital social force in the community, and it enjoyed the support of parents and nonparents alike. The group decided upon a project that was to have tremendous impact upon the educational endeavors of Negroes in Matagorda County. I still regard it as the most rewarding accomplishment of my Markham years. I do not recall how the idea was born, nor who the promoters were, but at some point it was decided that the PTA would raise fifty dollars and pay me to teach an extra month.

The money was raised by various and ingenious means. One event used to further the cause remains vividly in my memory: a box supper. To conduct this affair, young ladies brought beautifully decorated boxes filled with assorted delicacies. Young men then bought the boxes and each dined with the lady whose box he had purchased. Sometimes, to add to the drama of the occasion, the boxes were not identified and the purchaser could only hope that he had chosen the box he wanted. At other times the boxes bore identifications. Suspense on these occasions was assured if more than one young man had a strong desire to dine with a particular young lady. Then, if the contents of their pocketbooks matched the intensity of their longing, frantic bidding ensued. This was the situation that maintained on the night of our PTA box supper. When the bidding ended, my box had brought the magnificent sum of three dollars. Our receipts that night totaled slightly more than thirteen dollars, which was more than one-fourth of the ultimate goal.

Certainly the success of this financial effort provided the necessary motivation. I taught the seventh month and, at the end of April, a representative of the PTA brought me fifty dollars in coins and one-dollar bills tied in a man's soiled handkerchief. So the Negro youngsters of Markham had a seven-month school term in 1929-30. It was, I was told, the first time in the history of the school that the term had extended beyond six months. When I was asked by my trustee if I wanted the school for the next year, I replied with ill-concealed eagerness, "Yes, thank you."

The next year the PTA chose to repeat its previous project but, alas, the grip of the depression was so severe, raising a sum of fifty-five dollars proved to be an unrealistic goal. Only thirty dollars was raised, and I worked a seventh month for that sum. After all, the six-month term for which I had contracted expired at the end of March. Summer school did not begin until June. The possibility of my earning more than thirty dollars during those two intervening months was extremely remote. I reasoned that the additional month would be of benefit to the children and would in no way worsen my financial status.

I suppose the school board was either impressed with or embarrassed by the determined efforts of the PTA, for each of the two remaining terms of my tenure in Markham was of seven months' duration. The influence of these projects was not limited to that community. The impact was felt in Bay City, where the school for Negroes was staffed by a faculty of four who taught nine grades. There the citizens organized a PTA, raised funds, and paid the annual salary of an additional teacher. This practice was continued until the board included this item in its official budget.

During my last years at Markham, many schools paid their teachers with script that could be cashed at a discount, but until the end of my last pay period I was paid with checks negotiable at full value. When I went to pick up my last check at the end of the 1932-33 school year, I was told that I would either have to accept script or wait for a delayed check. I chose to wait. The check finally arrived in August, and we used it to make the initial payment on our present homesite.

When I left Markham in 1933, I had orally contracted to return for a fifth year, but developments of that summer caused a change in my plans and set the structure for new and more challenging teaching experiences.

3

EAST IS EAST AND
SOUTH IS SOUTH

*I*T WAS THREE YEARS now since that hot July afternoon when I furtively dashed from a seat beneath a live oak tree on the Prairie View College campus and joined Frank and the Reverend M. K. Barlow in the minister's Ford coupe. An hour later, I was addressed for the first time as Mrs. Robinson. The minister had conducted our marriage ceremony while we sat in his car parked beside a dirt road on the outskirts of Hempstead, Texas.

I had been properly "spoken for" as was the accepted social practice of that day. My parents had given their consent, and plans were being made for the wedding to take place immediately after Frank's graduation. But the impetuosity of young love, coupled with the stark fact that my parents could ill afford the cost of a wedding with all of the trappings, provided adequate reason for our unorthodox nuptial setting.

The three-year period since our marriage had brought significant changes in our lives. Frank had completed his work at Prairie View and was employed as the Negro County Agricultural Extension Agent for Anderson County with headquarters in Palestine. He was the first of that year's graduates from his department to receive employment. His director said the fact that Frank was married was in his favor, for marriage indicated some degree of maturity and stability. I continued to work in Markham and spent my summers with Frank in Palestine.

The economic condition of the country had worsened. The bank holiday of the early days of the Roosevelt administration was now

history. Whether any substantial improvement in the nation's economy had resulted from that effort was still being debated by bank-
ers, farmers, unemployed laborers, and others with little or no expertise in the field of economics. One thing was sure, however, and
that was the country certainly had in the White House a strong personality. The NRA, WPA, PWA, and other alphabetical entities
came into being. There was talk of what later became a reality—the
slaughtering of surplus cows and hogs, and the plowing under of
acres of cotton, potatoes, and tobacco. Soup lines lengthened,
freight trains hauled an increasing number of unemployed tran-
sients, and songwriters began to produce lyrics forecasting a better
time to come. Although we were caught up in the change, we were
among the more fortunate. We both suffered salary cuts, but at
least we were employed.

Since my visits were short, my contacts and observations were
superficial at best; but in spite of these limiting factors I was awed
by the contrasts between East Texas and South Texas. The natural
differences were marked. After years of living on dark, level land,
the red clay soil of Anderson County was a shock to me. The numerous gorges made bare by years of erosion saddened me, and
they do until this day. The pine trees were beautiful and strange
substitutes for the live oaks, mesquites, and cacti that I had known.
I even missed some of the birds and wildflowers of South Texas.

The symmetrical blocks of cultivated land with their artistic,
neat, straight rows of cotton or grain that I had known gave way
to small patches. Irregular rows, stumps, and even trees were common to cultivated areas in East Texas. Once during a visit, my
mother expressed her reaction to the contrast with, "If I lived here,
I am afraid I would plant a little patch of cotton or corn between
some of these pine groves and forget where it was."

The strangeness of my new home and my reaction to it in no
way indicate a dislike for East Texas. I have grown to like it very
much, to appreciate its beauty, and to recognize its natural resources
and advantages. After spending almost half a century here in East
Texas, it is impossible for me to say truthfully that I prefer one
part of the state to another.

The contrast between South Texas and East Texas was not limited to natural phenomena; the people were different too. In many respects, they were like neither the people in Lavaca County nor those in Matagorda County with whom I had worked. As a teacher these differences were of prime interest to me. I had ample opportunity to notice them, for my household responsibilities were few. We had a one-room apartment with cooking privileges, so I traveled with Frank almost daily during my summers, accompanying him on farm visits and to community meetings.

Most of Frank's clients were homeowners. They were people of great pride whose major goal was to be self supporting.

"Live at Home" was a slogan of the Extension Service at that time and to supply one's needs from his own farmstead was, in the opinion of most, an indication of respectability and good citizenship. In retrospect, it is impossible to determine whether this attitude was occasioned by nationwide deprivation resulting from the depression or a philosophy that had become a legacy. Reduced to its simplest terms, it actually meant survival, for there was none of the present-day governmental agencies to provide needed assistance. In the minds of most East Texas farmers, the live-at-home concept seemed to have had little relationship to shelter. That food should be given priority while shelter was of little concern may have been due to the economic conditions of the era or to the lack of appreciation for things other than the purely utilitarian.

Certainly there were those who could have afforded better housing; yet a comfortable, livable farm house was almost a rarity in Anderson County and this was doubly true in the black communities. Most houses were too small to accommodate the occupying families and were unscreened and unpainted. The addition of plumbing facilities, the provision for running water into a farm kitchen, or attempts at landscaping were considered newsworthy occurrences and often warranted release in the local newspaper, and surely such events formed a major part of the county agent's report.

These housing conditions were deplored greatly by Frank as he saw the farmers being exploited by large lumber companies that brought protable sawmills into the communities, bought the timber at ridiculously low prices, cut the pine trees, and moved on, leaving the farmer still in his shack with its leaking roof, its rotting sills, and its sagging porch.

That people lived in such dilapidated houses was understandable to me, for the poor people of South Texas also lived in seriously substandard housing, but I could not conceive of the apparent satisfaction or resignation on the part of the East Texan. Most of these people with whom Frank worked owned their homes, yet they made little effort toward their physical improvement, while the South Texan, even though he may have been a tenant, made some effort to enhance his living conditions. His efforts in this regard often consisted of no more than crudely attaching a rusty sheet of screen wire over the lower half of a window.

In his efforts to live at home, the more thrifty East Texas farmer produced a surplus that he readily exchanged for cash by peddling his supplies among the urban dwellers. I was awakened many mornings by the creak of a farmer's wagon accompanied by his clarion call, "Green peas already shelled." Housewives along the block, who gathered at his wagon, could not only buy the ready-shelled peas for ten cents per pint; they could choose from a variety of fresh vegetables, including potatoes, okra, beans, greens of various kinds, watermelons, cucumbers, and tomatoes. They might even acquire several pounds of fresh pork at ten cents per pound, or a choice cut of beef at a comparable price. All of this was legal for the city imposed no restrictive measures in this regard. If a housewife chose to purchase her steaks at a regular food market, she probably received a generous supply of stew meat or liver free.

Clothing prices were inconceivably low. I recall paying twenty-five cents at a J. C. Penny store for a two-piece cotton pique suit that served as a substantial part of my school wardrobe for two years.

There was still another noticeable difference in the people—intangible, but present nevertheless. This was their attitude toward intellectual improvement in general and in formal education specifically. There were seven black colleges within a one-hundred-mile radius of Palestine. In Anderson County alone, there were two high schools and more than forty ungraded smaller schools for blacks. Of this number, more than one-half were one-teacher schools. With these available educational facilities in mind, it was

a shock and a surprise for me to learn that the percentage of illiter-
acy was higher in Anderson County than in Matagorda County.
This was true of both the black population and the whites.

There seemed to be a lack of motivation, especially among the
black people. They lived with what might have been justifiably
called the "Messiah concept"—that salvation would be brought to
them, that help and improvement of an intellectual nature would
come from some external source, and that it would be miraculously
administered. Many communities had their local heroes—native
sons who had grown up "right here on these clay hills," and had
gone away to achieve renown as teachers or ministers and, in a few
cases, as physicians or lawyers. These were referred to with admi-
ration and awesome respect, but the feeling and knowledge that
these achievements could be duplicated seemed to be far fetched
or totally lacking.

Any attempt to analyze and understand this dearth of ambition
should be accompanied by recognition of the fact that ambition
must be nurtured, and the people of this locality were suffering
from a severe lack of the catalytic influences necessary to the nurturing process. No telephones or hard-surfaced roads served the
average rural community. Farm-to-market roads were nonexistent,
and only two highways crossed the county. To undertake automobile travel on most of the county roads after a heavy rain was to
undertake the impossible. Of course, automobiles were few, but
the task of traveling over these roads was not easy for a mule team.
Conditions of this nature imposed an isolation upon the people and
caused each community to function more or less as a social entity
unto itself. Even adjacent communities maintained little contact
with each other.

There were two annual occasions, however, that were exceptions.
These were School Closing and Big Meeting. To present a public
program to mark the end of the school term was a common practice, and a disregard for this tradition was viewed as being near
criminal. These public school closing programs that consisted
mainly of speeches, orations, plays, drills, monologues, and singing,
were so important that in spite of limited means of communication,
teachers of the various schools somehow managed to schedule their

program dates in such a manner that there would be no conflicts. Friday nights were the preferred time but, to make inter-community attendance possible, many programs were held on earlier week nights.

School Closing was indeed the gala social event of the year and, although perhaps only a few of those concerned recognized it as such, it was an experience of great image-building potential. As unjust as it might have been, many teachers were evaluated on the quality of the closing program that she presented. Little wonder then, that a "closing practice period" became an important item on the daily schedule during the last month or even the last six weeks of the school term. That the total length of the school session was only six or seven months did not in any way alter this practice.

Parents found in the school closing programs two media through which they could bolster their self-image. To be able to deck their youngsters out in new clothing gave some testimony to the family's economic status. Then if the children performed their parts well, the parents had the added pleasure of publicly proving that they had produced superior progeny.

The young participants on the program had an opportunity to display their skill as orators, actors, or singers, and though no formal awards were given, there was generally in each community someone who earned the reputation of being the "best in the country." This designation was worn until the honored individual dropped out of school or a more talented person was discovered.

"Big Meeting" was a term I have heard only in East Texas. It is held in the summer usually during the month of July or August and either marks the beginning or the culmination of the annual church revival meeting. It was, and still is, a multifaceted occasion. It is a homecoming, a fashion show, a food fair, a lover's paradise, and an exhibition of religious emotionalism. A feat of this magnitude demands the weeks of planning and preparation that it duly receives. There is always talk of who is coming home from Dallas, Houston, Fort Worth, Chicago, or Los Angeles; what delicacies the ladies of the community will include in their dinner boxes; the amount of money that is being spent on the Big Meeting costume of certain of the local belles, and what visiting pastors are expected to preach.

I shall always remember the wonderment I knew as I watched my mother-in-law prepare for the first Big Meeting that I attended in Frank's home community. She removed the entire contents from a huge turret-top trunk and lined the inside with newspapers, followed by a scrupulously white cloth. Then she carefully placed inside, the products of her culinary skill, the preparation of which had taken the greater part of the previous day. There was a huge beef roast, several baked hens, fried chicken, cakes, pies and cobblers of various kinds, potato salad, boiled cabbage, and boiled beans.

Underneath the shade trees on the church grounds, a long table had been improvised by the "brothers" of the church. Each "sister" pridefully placed tasteful portions from her box at each place setting along the table. Bowls of salad and other succulent dishes were placed at intervals along the entire length of the table. The cry, "Dinner is served" was the welcome invitation for all present to come and dine.

After contributing her share of food to the long visitors' table, it was a common practice of most of the ladies to hold a few delicacies in reserve and invite special friends and relatives to "Come by my box." Failure to respond favorably to this invitation was often considered an affront, especially if the invited guest had been seen, or was seen later, partaking of food from another box. In my early years I was careful to offend no one by failing to honor the come-by-my-box invitation. My ability to issue a polite regret was not born until I saw Frank suffer a painful digestive disturbance that resulted from eating improperly refrigerated chicken dressing at a Big Meeting dinner.

Where there is lack of communication, there is lack of knowledge, and where there is lack of knowledge there is fear. Perhaps in no aspect of human existence is this more profound than in the area of race relations. I do not know if racial barriers were more rigid in East Texas than in South Texas, but it seems to me they were. It could be by the time I came to East Texas I had reached a stage of maturity that made me more sensitive to the whole spectrum of race relations. Anyway, rigid barriers did exist, and the perpetration of these barriers in East Texas was implemented by overt and drastic means.

When we came to Palestine, there was still fresh in the minds of the black population an incident in which respectable black men and women had been beaten away from the polls with ax handles and some had been placed in jail. Equally fresh in their memory were the horrors of a race riot in Slocum that had erupted a few years previously. These stories were related to us in hushed tones accompanied by a weird mixture of deep-seated bitterness, smoldering anger, and helpless surrender.

I know now that Frank and I were spared many of the gross embarrassments that the menially-employed blacks experienced with recurrent frequency. But we, too, had more than our share. There was the time when, in his capacity as county agent, Frank was in a planning meeting for the Anderson County Fair, then known as the Texas Fruit Palace. None of the buildings on the fairgrounds was equipped with plumbing, and separate toilets were a legal fact. There was a toilet for white women, and when Frank requested similar accommodations for black women, the fair manager replied, "Let them go to the woods; that is what they are used to." The memory of that statement was always an open emotional sore for Frank.

Because Frank's sphere of operation was broader than mine, he probably experienced more embarrassing encounters of this nature than I did, but I was by no means immune. Still vivid in my memory is the occasion when I was refused a ticket for a free drawing, even though the amount of my purchase qualified me for participation in the daily drawing that was being conducted by a local drugstore. When I requested the ticket, the owner told me quite emphatically yet not unkindly, "I'm sorry, but in this town, colored people do not participate in drawings." I replied with equal emphasis, "I'm sorry, but this will be the last purchase I'll make at this store." And it was, as long as he retained ownership. His attitude, however, was purely personal and did not represent any city-wide policy.

So in East Texas during the early 1930s, white was white and black was black and never the twain met on common ground, even though both groups experienced common sufferings, many of which were spawned by economic deprivation and by intellectual stagnation.

4

DESERT BLOSSOMS

*I*T WAS A DAY in late August, 1933, and the heavy heat discouraged even the most moderate activity. The leaves of the trees were reduced to a lazy stillness. Few birds made aerial ventures through the dusty foliage of the sweet gums, elms, catalpas, and pines that outlined the dirt road we were traveling. Occasionally a droning insect would wander into the open 1932 V-8 Ford and threaten both my safety and my sanity. It took more than dust, heat, and migrant insects to dull our youthful enthusiasm, for we had never heard of an air-conditioned automobile; we were in love, and moreover, Frank was taking me to Pine Hill, a community nine miles from Palestine I had never visited before.

After covering some eight miles of serpentine roadway, much of which was rimmed by steep clay banks, we reached a hill. The only visible road leading to the peak was little more than a bridle path, but Frank forced the little car over the stumps, along deep, dry ruts, and past clutching vines that scratched the shiny surface of the sides of the car. Suddenly there it was—the school house where the community meeting was to be held. It was a one-room affair similar in general structure to the buildings in which I had worked in Matagorda and Lavaca counties. It could claim the same bare ugliness, but it had one distinguishing feature, and that was the double front door that marked its single entrance.

The building in no way arrested my attention, but the campus did. It was unforgettable. To this day, I remember my exact words which were, "I'd surely hate to teach here; just look at that campus." To persons who are accustomed to the modern landscape treatment of today's school grounds, my description of the Wellersberg and Markham school campuses must sound incredible, but they were like the gardens of Versailles compared to what I now beheld. There was scarcely four square feet of yard surface that was safe for play. The building was located on a site that had been cleared of a pine grove, with many stumps left standing, like gravestones, two or three feet high.

Perhaps man's inadequacies are best documented by his lack of prescience and that his mortal inconsistencies are more easily forgiven when one considers the variables with which he is forced to deal. So in spite of my aversion to the Pine Hill School campus, a few weeks after my first visit I signed a contract to teach there for fifty dollars per month for six months. The signing of that contract was a happy occasion for me, because it meant that Frank and I would no longer be separated by the 250 miles between Palestine and Markham, a distance that seemed interminable at that time. It also meant the beginning of my teaching career in East Texas—a career that would end in the same county forty-one years later.

If teaching in South Texas had been a challenge, my new position demanded a compulsion. The youngsters who came to me in the fall of 1933 seemed to need everything—improved nutrition, clothing, basic academic instruction, motivation to dream of a better life, and, perhaps most important of all, a sense of individual worth and personal dignity.

If structured community planning was a common practice of that period, it had completely escaped me. I did not even map out an informal procedure for meeting the community needs. I suppose an accurate statement would be that simultaneous attacks were made on many fronts. Recalling my success with the PTA in Markham, one of my first acts was to perfect organization of the PTA at Pine Hill.

Since the stumps on the campus were a bane to my emotional health, campus improvement was one of our earliest efforts. Being the wife of the county agent gave me an advantage. The Farmers Community Council, motivated by the cooperative spirit of the Extension Service, joined with the PTA in planning Campus Improvement Days. This cooperation was easily secured, for most of the community's citizens were members of both organizations. Actually, the Campus Improvement Days became gala events. The men appeared early with spades, axes, hoes, scoops, scrapers, and mule teams. The housewives appeared later with lunch boxes, the contents of which rivaled the gourmet offerings of a Big Meeting basket.

There were a few citizens whose advanced age prevented their active participation, but they came anyway and smiled their pride and approval while, at recess, the children scampered about in a new-found sense of self importance. After all, was not all of this being done for them?

Soon the Pine Hill School campus was smooth and bare of unsightly stumps. It might be truthfully added that it was bare of everything else, as there were no ornamental plantings and no playground equipment. It is not a matter of personal pride for me to admit that, when I left Pine Hill fours years later, the campus was still void of these attributes with one exception and that was a seesaw crudely made of native pine slabs. This is not to say, however, that we did not enjoy campus activities. The leveled ground made possible the laying out of a baseball diamond and an area for track and field events.

The personal appearance of many of my students posed another problem. How could I tackle such a sensitive area without incurring the resentment of the parents and damaging the child's self image, an image that I was trying so desperately to enhance? Through general appeals, encouragement, and compliments when such was warranted, I soon developed a kind of rapport that enabled me to tell a child frankly in private to take a bath or launder his clothing before returning to school the next day. In dealing with a few stubborn cases, I resorted to combing hair, sewing on buttons, and cutting tatters from ragged sleeves and the legs of union suits. To my knowledge, not one parent ever protested or objected in any way to my ventures into these very private areas.

The language of these East Texas youngsters was a source of interest to me as well as a source of confusion in some instances. Certainly the language of the children whom I had taught in South

Texas was no model of grammatical purity, but there were terms common in East Texas that I simply did not understand. I had never heard the word "freshening"; consequently, when a young boy said, "Mama sent you some freshening," my facial expression revealed my lack of comprehension. How was I to know that the family had recently butchered a hog, and that the mother was expressing the family's high regard for me by sending me a generous supply of spare ribs and pork chops? In similar manner, when a boy's reply to a request was "Wall'um," I was totally lacking in understanding. His sister provided the necessary interpretation when she said, "Mrs. Robinson, he is going to do what you told him to do." Frank later led me to know that "Wall'um" really meant "Well, ma'am."

The lack of nutritious diets was by no means restricted to East Texas. It existed to some degree on a nationwide scale, but it was intensified in the South, and it prompted reference by President Roosevelt in his famous pronouncement that, "One third of this nation is ill-housed, ill-clothed, and ill-fed." Free school lunches were unheard of in our section of the country, and I doubt that there was a rural school in Anderson County that had any provision for the preparation and serving of hot lunches, for their families butchered their own hogs and produced an ample supply of cane syrup. Pork and syrup accompanied by large home-baked biscuits comprised the typical school lunch. While this fare was far short of being a nutritious and balanced meal, it was better than many fall and spring lunches that consisted mainly of syrup and bread only. Later, using the Pine Hill community as a basis for study, I did my undergraduate thesis, "Food Habits and Health Conditions in a Rural Community in Anderson County, Texas." My thesis, rated by the home economics faculty at Prairie View as one of the better studies of that period, was placed in the college library.

Daily I looked at my malnourished students and needled myself with the thought that the responsibility for alleviating the situation was mine. I promised myself that next year something must be done, and it was.

Our county was one of the few in Texas that had the services of a Jeanes supervisor. I do not know how counties qualified for this service, but I do know that the title was derived from the fact the Jeanes-Slater Fund provided a part of the salaries of these supervisors, and I believe their services were limited to black schools. Anyway, our Jeanes supervisor, Miss Sophia E. Montgomery, an energetic young woman, seemed to have an inexhaustible store of innovative ideas. One of them embodied a strategy for providing hot lunches for rural school children. Her plan was crude and simple and I accepted it enthusiastically. After a long search of restaurants, boarding houses, and filling stations, I obtained a five-gallon container with a lid. When I appeared at the school house with my newly acquired possession, my children were naturally curious, and I told them we were going to have hot lunches every school day. I then explained the procedure. Each day we would put about three inches of water in our big pot, set it on the heater, and the children would place their small jars of food in it. The same energy that heated the classroom would warm our lunches. Then at noon each child would have a jar of hot food. Daily the children brought their jars of beans, peas, potatoes, corn, greens, pears, peaches, and berries. Placing the odd assortment in our big pot became such an important task for the older boys and girls that it was necessary to develop a rotating schedule so each one could have his day of glory. Crude though this attempt was, it represented a concrete effort to improve the nutritional status of the students, and to some degree it succeeded.

The first Interscholastic League meet for rural school children in Anderson County was held in the mid-1930s. Seeing in this activity another opportunity for my students to enhance their self-image, I planned to take part. Our leveled campus now proved its worth. We laid out track lanes and improvised equipment for vaulting, high jumping, hurdling, and broad jumping. Knowing the competition among the various schools would be keen, we began practicing weeks prior to the league meet. Our recess periods were devoted to such a variety of athletic activities that our campus took on the semblance of a miniature Olympic meet.

All of our energies were not devoted to athletic endeavors. Spellers, declaimers, storytellers, and number-sense contestants were being trained with equal dedication. Practice for these literary contests was integrated with the regular language-arts and arithmetic programs, and thereby did little to disrupt the daily schedule.

A competitive spirit was easily developed and the desire to win soon reached high intensity, but then other problems surfaced. Some of my best athletes were girls, and the matter of costumes suitable for effective athletic performance proved to be controversial. In the 1930s it was not a common practice for people to appear in public in shorts. Voluminous bloomers were generally worn by girls when they engaged in any form of physical exercise. I knew that bloomers would impede the activities of my girls, but some of my most supportive parents thought the wearing of shorts was the epitome of immodesty, and they had no intention of allowing their daughters to do it.

A solution was reached when the PTA agreed on a compromise: a three-piece costume done in the school colors and consisting of white blouse, lavendar shorts, and wraparound skirt. The skirts were to be removed only when the girls were actually competing. The cloth was bought in bolts and each family paid its pro rata share. The garments were cut out at school under the teacher's supervision, and a few mothers with reasonable sewing skill did the actual construction.

Another problem was transportation. How was I to get my contestants to the meet? Our car was one-seated, the parents had none. Few indeed were school buses in Anderson County at that time. There was only one school bus for blacks, the product of the joint effort of an enterprising agriculture teacher and a manual-arts teacher who had built the bed in the school shop and installed it on a second-hand chassis. As the league meet drew near, my problem remained unsolved; then the answer came to me one Sunday morning in church. My thoughts went to a man who owned a lumber truck and, when I contacted him, he consented to provide our needed transportation. So the students and teacher of Pine Hill School went to the meet on a lumber truck with sideboards attached for safety. It was a great day for the contestants, the boosters, the spectators, and the teacher. Winning honors in both literary and athletic events, we had several ribbons to attest to our superiority. Casual observers saw the ribbons and were curious; the parents saw them and were proud. When I looked at the ribbons I saw children with new pride.

Now teaching at my third school, I had yet to find a single library book at a school when I came, and I had never left one when I departed. I was hopeful of removing this negative aspect of my teaching record. But how? Again, the resourcefulness of our Jeanes supervisor proved to be my salvation. She informed me of a plan through which a school could secure a small library by participating in a special program provided by the Rosenwald Foundation. I do not know the exact conditions a school had to meet to qualify for this aid but, if it meant economic deprivation, our school probably was overqualified. Anyway, according to our supervisor, we could acquire the Rosenwald Library along with a bookcase for twenty-five dollars. As I recall, the library consisted of an assortment of twenty-five or thirty books. The only titles that I remember are *Heidi* and *The Swiss Family Robinson*.

To raise the required sum, I asked each family to give fifty cents. Most families responded, but some could give only twenty-five cents, some even less. This proved to be no real hardship however, because a few friends in town added their donations to mine. Soon a collection of new, colorful, interesting books graced our crowded classroom. It was a source of great satisfaction to me to watch the excitement with which many of the students used our library.

The autonomy of the small school during my early teaching years is still a mystery to me. I do not know if there was a lack of governmental regulations such as those that provide today's guidelines for school operation, or whether such guidelines existed and I was never apprised of them. Perhaps the extreme flexibility that characterized the operation of such schools was simply another indication that a small rural school for blacks in the 1930s was in essence a nonentity and did not merit major consideration of any type.

I do know that I was a rather free agent and did just about what I wanted to do, as long as I did not ask for anything that would entail the expenditure of money. My freedom was complete in such areas as subjects and number of grades taught and the size of enrollment. This freedom, combined with my over zeal to help as many children as I could in all possible ways, resulted in a severe personal frustration.

Whether or not it was justified, my reputation as a "good teacher" spread to adjacent communities and some parents who lived reasonably close to Pine Hill began to withdraw their children from their own school and send them to ours. There was never any question about the propriety or the legality of such action. The children would simply appear and ask to be enrolled and, with equal innocence and naivete, I would enroll them.

The impact of this free enrollment practice struck me with debilitating force one late winter morning in 1935 when I found myself facing a room of sixty-three squirming bodies ranging in age from seven to seventeen and enrolled in grades one through seven. The sixty-three individuals represented sixty-three challenges and demands. I had no means of measuring intelligence or inventorying interests, but I knew there was a wide range of both. My best attempt at a daily schedule resulted in a series of ten-minute class periods. The whole situation was most discouraging. Even now, I recall that day as the time my teaching spirit was lowest. Certainly in the years that followed I knew many disappointments and suffered intense frustrations, but I have experienced nothing that matched the emptiness and abysmal despair of that day.

During the noon hour, after the lunches had been eaten and while the children played unsupervised, I sat beneath a pine tree and cried like a three-year-old. Somehow, as if by some line of divine communication that opened while the tears flooded my cheeks, the one logical solution came to me, amazing in its simplicity. Why had I not thought of it before? The answer obviously was addition of another room and another teacher. I wonder now if my knowledge of the general reluctance of school officials to spend money on black schools had caused me to suppress this thought from my consciousness. Once the idea was born, I began to plot my strategy. Explaining it to the PTA members, I planned a special public program honoring the superintendent and members of the board of education.

On the night of the program, the honored guests were present, as were the parents and other interested citizens. All seats were filled and many stood in the narrow aisles along the rough walls. The youngsters performed superbly as they "said their speeches," acted their parts in playlets, and participated in group singing.

I composed a rhyme dedicated to and extolling the virtues of the superintendent. Actually the content focused more on what we hoped he would do than what he had done. This verse was recited by a little girl who was quite skilled in declaiming, having won a ribbon at the league meet to prove it. Her rendition was so beautifully done that everything that followed was anticlimactic, and this included the school officials' promise to comply with our request for an additional room and an additional teacher.

This promise was not without certain conditions. The school board would provide the lumber for the new room and would pay the head carpenter and the painter. The men of the community would provide free labor as carpenter helpers, and the PTA would pay for the paint. These conditions met with general approval.

So the Pine Hill School opened in October, 1935 with an additional room and one more teacher. The new room, attached to the old one, simply made the building longer. It stood in striking ugliness, the unpainted newness of one room contrasting sharply with the soiled painted siding of the other. This was soon remedied, however, as a member of the board owned a general store and provided the paint with the understanding that the bill could be paid when the PTA raised the money. The total amount was about sixty dollars.

The new teacher was Miss Edna J. Tillis, a brilliant, attractive, personable young woman who had recently graduated from Mary Allen Junior College. She was assigned to teach grades one through four. Since the board made no provision for students to be transferred to other districts for training beyond the seventh grade, and since parents were unable to provide private transportation for that purpose, I exercised the freedom of adding another grade and assigned myself the responsibility of teaching grades five through eight.

The choice of Miss Tillis was mine, and from the beginning it proved to be a wise one. She promptly gained the love and respect of parents and children, and her efforts in helping the PTA to raise money to pay for the paint demonstrated her resourcefulness.

The PTA plan to meet its financial obligation took the form of a sort of popularity contest; the contestant who raised the larger sum of money was declared the winner and appropriately rewarded. Miss Tillis was chosen to sponsor one young girl, I another. Relatives, friends, and students chose the contestant they wished to support. Each contestant and her supporters were free to raise funds in whatever manner they chose.

We soon discovered a unique and lucrative source of income that both Miss Tillis and I used extensively. At that time most homes in Palestine were heated by wood, and kindling was a prime necessity. Fat pine was one of the best kindling materials, and many homeowners secured it from farmers who peddled from door to door. Once we made our objective known, we cornered much of that market. We teachers booked orders in town and transferred these orders to our students who relayed them to their parents. The next day boys and girls would come to school with their books in one arm and a bundle of pine kindling in the other. The proceeds from each sale were credited to the contestant the bearer was supporting. These sales from ten- and twenty-five-cent bundles of pine, combined with the sale of holly and other greenery for Christmas decoration, enabled us to pay off our indebtedness much sooner than we had anticipated.

Incidentally, Miss Tillis's protégé won the contest and was given a wristwatch. My girl received a gift of appreciation. This feat served to strengthen the community's regard for the new teacher and, as best I could discern, it did nothing to harm my image.

All told, we were a happy group of people, because we were doing something meaningful and working cooperatively a long time before the term "togetherness" had earned its place of current popularity.

With the hiring of the second teacher, whose salary was set at fifty dollars per month, my salary was raised to sixty-five dollars per month. Miss Tillis and I paid fourteen dollars each per month for daily taxi service to and from school. This was a happy change for me. During my first year at Pine Hill, Frank took me to and from work each day, but this arrangement proved very disruptive of his schedule and often subjected me to long waits after school; so during the second year, I roomed in the community and boarded myself, coming home on weekends. The privilege of coming home at the end of each day and exchanging professional experiences proved to be as fulfilling as we had anticipated. This sharing of professional problems, concerns, and ideas became a sort of ritual with us and is one that we have observed through the years.

I resigned from the Pine Hill School to accept a position with a fraternal insurance company that paid me sixty dollars per month, plus two dollars per diem and travel expenses when I was obliged to work out of town. In considering the change, finance was our only concern. We had just built the home in which we now live, and an increase in the family income was both needed and welcome.

Many of my students at Pine Hill have long since left this area, and I have completely lost contact with them. There are others whom I see or hear from regularly. There is the middle-aged alcoholic, now a grandfather, whom I meet on the street occasionally. He invariably passes me a dime and says, "Here, Mrs. Robinson, buy yourself something for all of the trouble I used to give you." In retrospect, I am tempted to think of him as one of the two most nearly incorrigible students I ever worked with. On the other hand, I remember many of my Pine Hill students with pride. There is the man who went directly into military service out of high school, gained the rank of colonel, retired, graduated from the University of California, and now owns and operates a thriving real estate business in the Bay area. It was he who paid me public tribute upon my retirement by relating my influence on his life and by comparing me to the teacher in the movie, "Sounder."

I think with equal pride of the bank teller in Los Angeles, the store manager in a small southern California town, the public school teacher in South Texas, the nursery school supervisor in Houston, the several civil-service workers, beauticians, and the two ministers. By virtue of my long residence in Anderson County, I have had the opportunity to know the children of some of my Pine Hill students, and to note their accomplishments. I refer to these as my professional grandchildren, and it has been both interesting and gratifying to note the large number of this group that have gone to college or have pursued technical training and have thus responded to the increase in job options that are now open to blacks.

One of the most profound satisfactions of my retirement years is the feeling that some early dreams fashioned from the gossamer threads of my youth have been transformed into concrete realities in terms of a better life for people. Seeds that were scattered among the stumps and underneath the pines a generation ago are still yielding a beautiful human harvest. This, after all, is the hoped-for goal of all teachers for it is the essence of teaching. The philosophy that sustains a teacher is based on the knowledge that all does not end with each day's effort when the bell rings at four.

5

DRY MORSELS

At TWENTY-EIGHT YEARS of age, I was leaving the teaching profession. I had earned the baccalaureate degree and had nine years of teaching experience, yet my annual salary had never exceeded $450. As low as this figure was, my salary was by no means unusual for that day. Rather, it was probably average for black rural teachers of East Texas. This low salary scale should not be viewed in isolation as one peculiar aspect of the educational picture. It was, in fact, symptomatic of the deplorable status of the total spectrum of public education in East Texas.

Admittedly, teachers generally were poorly prepared academically. Most of the black teachers were working on temporary certification. A few held the "lifetime permanent" certificate that embodied language to the effect that the holder was "hereby certified to teach all grades in the public schools of the state of Texas throughout his natural life." When I began teaching in Anderson County, the number of black teachers who held the baccalaureate degree was less than twelve. White teachers probably could claim no higher percentage, but it was years later when professional interchange between the races became a common practice that I discovered this. When desegregation was effected in East Texas, it was a surprise to many to find that the percentage of black teachers who held master's degrees exceeded that of whites.

The subterfuge, intrigue, and unethical practices in the hiring of teachers will never be fully revealed. Such transactions are, for obvious reasons, cloaked in secrecy. But there could never be any concealment of the fact that the daughter or the son of a black woman who worked as a domestic in the home of a member of the Board of Education was readily added to the teaching staff. By the same token, the wife of a black custodian or a railroad porter rarely found any difficulty in being hired to fill a teaching position.

Another demoralizing procedure in hiring teachers was the outright sale of contracts. One man brazenly explained to me his extensive operation in an adjacent county. At the end of each school year, he paid the county superintendent for several blank contracts. He then sold these contracts to black teachers at a considerable profit. He generally charged the equivalent of one month's salary. The necessary cooperation of the superintendent was of course assured.

The practice of paying for teaching positions became remarkably sophisticated. Sometimes it was the superintendent who received a rebate from a teacher, or a group of teachers, each payday. In other instances, financial arrangements were made with board members. Alliances were formed whereby each teacher paid a certain trustee. The teacher was then known as "his teacher," and the trustee was referred to as "his trustee" or "her trustee." Occasionally the principal was the recipient of these extralegal fees. Whether he shared this fund with his superiors depended entirely upon the terms of the agreement.

Another fairly common ruse was to ask teachers if they would express their loyalty to the district and to the cause of education by contributing to the cost of a gymnasium, a science laboratory, or for some other facility for which there was an obvious need. The quoted price of these projects was always in excess of the actual figure. Since no auditor's report or any kind of financial statement was ever released, and since the teachers always felt "loyal," such efforts were always well supported.

I do not know if the merchandising of teacher contracts was as extensive among whites as it was among blacks, but I do know that many teachers paid for their jobs in one way or another. Many times my friends have expressed disbelief when I stated that I taught in East Texas for thirty-six years and never paid for a job. On one occasion, however, I was requested to pay.

Some districts maintained subtrustees. These were black men who were regarded as leaders in their communities and were supposedly sensitive to, and interested in the welfare of black people. They were responsible to the elected trustees, who were generally white. The subtrustees selected the black teacher and relayed their choice to the official board members who completed the legal transaction of hiring the teacher. I was interested in a position in a district where all the subtrustees were farmers. When I went for an interview, I found each one plowing in his field. So the interview resulted in work stoppage for a few minutes for each of the three. I was duly recommended and was hired. After my contract was signed, the three men came to Frank in a body and explained that they felt the time spent away from plowing during the interview was "worth a little something." Frank consented that perhaps their point of view had some merit, but when they quoted thirty dollars as an acceptable figure, Frank had some second thoughts. Since the interview with each lasted about ten minutes, they were asking a figure that was comparable to a wage scale of sixty dollars per hour at a time when two dollars per day was considered reasonable and equitable. Moreover, thirty dollars was approximately 10 percent of my contracted annual pay. We entertained no intention of paying the thirty dollars, but we both knew that my tenure at that school would be limited to one year. So when I had an opportunity to go to Pine Hill, I asked to be released from my contract.

Without too much probing, the superintendent granted my request. She tore up the contract in my presence. I felt a sense of moral relief and profound gratitude as I watched the tattered bits of paper fall into her wastebasket.

One method employed by teachers to maintain tenure was to serve members of the board or their friends in various menial capacities, or to work on similar jobs during summer vacations. I still recall the shock I knew when an experienced teacher several years my senior visited Tyler, Texas, one weekend, and upon returning said, "I saw my first college." This is not to say that she was teaching under false credentials. Her certificate was no doubt valid and she may have earned it attending "summer normals," tak-

ing extension courses, or "passing the county board." Passing the
county board consisted of supplying the correct answers to a given
number of questions related to such basic areas as mathematics,
geography, hygiene, literature, civics, and grammar. I am not sure
who developed the questions, but the examination was usually giv-
en under the supervision of the superintendent or some other person of equal educational rank.

Since the practical merits of any system are determined by the
honesty of those who engage in it, the county board examinations
occasionally suffered corruption. If a participant failed to pass the
test, some officials would gladly remedy the situation when an attractive sum of money was made visible. Other corruptive devices
were sometimes employed. I heard one elderly teacher tell, without shame or remorse, how she had taken the county board in the
name of her daughter. She of course passed the test, and the daughter began teaching at the age of fifteen. Fortunately the young
teacher grew in the profession and enjoyed many years as a successful teacher. She is presently retired and draws a monthly check
from the Texas Retirement System of Texas.

Summer normals had ceased to operate by the time I entered the
teaching profession, but extension classes were rather commonplace. They provided a great convenience for teachers who sought
in-service improvement or for those who were working for higher
certification. Furthermore, a limited number of hours earned in
extension classes could be transferred to degree programs. By taking advantage of these extension courses and by attending summer
school as resident students, the number of teachers holding baccalaureate degrees began to increase slowly.

Many years were yet to pass before a black teacher in Anderson
County received a master's degree. The reason is obvious. There
was not a black institution in the state in the 1930s that offered
programs on that level, and there was not a white institution that
admitted blacks. If a black teacher insisted on this higher training,
he was obliged to attend an institution in another state. If requested, by special arrangement, the state of Texas would pay the
fees. This practice continued until legal action brought by blacks
in the late forties resulted in the reluctant dissolution of racial bar-

riers in the state supported institutions of higher learning.

Fortified by and delighted with this long-denied right and convenience, I registered at the University of Texas in the summer of 1955, the first black woman from Anderson County to do so. Incidentally, the first two black women from Anderson County to graduate from the University of Texas were former students of mine, and the third to was a member of my staff.

By the time I entered the University of Texas, I had already earned a master's degree from San Francisco State Teachers College and, in the pursuit thereof, had driven more than ten thousand miles by automobile, traveling all night on three or four occasions; had been denied motel accommodations in Nevada, breakfast in Salt Lake City, and had been refused a cup of coffee at two o'clock in the morning in a Wyoming coffee shop.

In the early 1930s the average black teacher's contract was for six months, but this did not always determine the exact length of the school term. Occasionally a week or two were added and, conversely, sometimes the term was shortened by a few days or weeks. Evidently, prior notice of reduced terms was not considered important. The superintendent felt no qualms about informing a teacher, "Your school will close next Friday." If he felt that his actions warranted any explanation whatsoever, he simply said, "The money has run out." For a teacher to protest in any fashion was unheard of and, I suspect, unthought of. In one instance a teacher was not notified that "the money has run out," and when the superintendent did establish contact with her, he said, "Your school closed last Friday." I never learned what financial adjustment was made in this case.

Another example of the flexibility in teachers' contracts was a situation in which each of two teachers was given a contract to teach the same one-teacher school. I have never known how this confusing and embarrassing condition developed. During the first few days of the school term, the teacher who arrived at the building first was the teacher for that day. It naturally became a race between the two to see who could arrive first. Fortunately for all concerned, the younger of the two received a call to a position in West Texas. She accepted, and spent many years as a successful teacher and is now enjoying retirement.

All of the demoralizing forces that affected professionalism among black educators by no means external. The internal structure of their relationship was within itself a debilitating influence. City teachers—those who taught in the Palestine Independent School District—were generally thought to regard themselves as superior to their rural counterparts. Whether or not these teachers actually entertained such an image of themselves, the result was the same. There was little professional communication between the two groups.

This feeling was intensified when, under the leadership of the Jeanes supervisor and Paul L. Rutledge (the principal of the only rural high school), all teachers of the county were called together to organize the Anderson County Teachers Association. Although representatives from the city schools attended the meeting, they would not accept membership in the new organization. According to their spokesman, it was felt "the needs and problems of the city schools differed too greatly from those of the rural schools." That was in 1934, and throughout the intervening years I have tried to discover the vast difference the spokesman of that day professed to see.

It was a decade later that the City Teachers Association was organized, but the Anderson County Teachers Association grew and flourished. It was among the first professional groups in the county to qualify for membership in the National Education Association (NEA).

The basis for the superior attitude the city teachers were thought to possess posed a great mystery to the rural teachers, for by and large, the rural teachers were more highly trained academically; and with the advent of state aid for some of the more financially deprived districts, many rural teachers received better pay. One city teacher once told me that her annual salary was $540 and that she was paid in twelve equal payments, thus making her monthly check amount to $45.

I have often wondered if this intellectual snobbery, the professional caste system, was not covertly encouraged by the white administration to further the concept of "divide and conquer." Anyway, many years passed and many districts were consolidated before there was any appreciable unification between these two groups.

The black teachers of that period worked under the corruptive influence of a montage of negative factors including low salaries, short school terms, inadequate facilities and equipment, legal restrictions, administrative apathy, overt bribery, mediocre training, and professional disunity. With this in mind, it is almost inevitable that one would conclude that any teaching that took place must have been of very poor quality. But this was not always the case. Many of those teachers taught with a zeal and dedication that is rarely in evidence today. It was as though they felt a personal mandate to compensate for the areas of lack in the lives of their students. There was a cosmopolitan quality to their approach. They possessed the rare ability to believe—to keep the torch of faith burning in their own lives—and were able, therefore, to light a torch in the lives of others. They were living, breathing examples of the fact that expensive hardware, imposing architecture, and even advanced training do not necessarily make for successful teaching— that the greatest change that takes place in any classroom results from the impact of student-teacher relationships.

Perhaps because most black teachers come from a low socioeconomic environment, they can easily identify with the majority of America's children, for most of America's children are not rich.

Since integration, this quality of the black teacher has gained considerable visibility. A white teacher on my staff referred to it one day when she said, "I believe black teachers, as a group, are warmer than white teachers; at least they express more warmth toward the children." I tended to agree, remembering with nostalgia the black teachers of a generation ago who "made brick without straw."

6

NEW WINE

I CANNOT SAY THAT my employment with the insurance company was without reward, for I very thoroughly enjoyed some aspects of the work. I like people, and the cultivation of relationships with people was the basis for success. When I resigned, my district was leading all others in a jurisdiction comprising twenty-three states and the District of Columbia. So I can justifiably claim success in the fraternal-insurance field. There was one negative factor, however, and that was the monotony of visiting repeatedly the same small East Texas towns.

Job security remained the decisive consideration. Financial consideration, having caused me to leave teaching in the first place, would figure significantly in my return.

One day, as though by providential design and certainly without any effort on my part, I received an invitation from the county superintendent to come for a job interview. His offer of employment in a state-aid school with a salary of $106.50 per month for a nine-month period was very attractive. Here was an opportunity to free myself from the dull trips that had become loathesome. Here was an opportunity to live at home and, most appealing of all, to return to my beloved teaching. I had never denied either to myself or others that I missed the contact with school people.

I discussed quite candidly my ambivalence about changing jobs. In my interview with the superintendent, I stressed the high priority I placed on financial security. I cannot explain, even to this day, why I felt so strongly about sustained income. I never feared being fired from a job, and I never was; but always gnawing in the background of my consciousness was an awareness that people were unemployed, and that I could allow myself to be one of them.

The superintendent was kind enough to assure me that as long as he was in office I would have my desired security. I gambled. I trusted him and accepted the position.

I was assigned to Lost Prairie School, which was another one-teacher facility, but the building was far superior to any in which I had worked before. At one time, it had housed two teachers. It was known as a Rosenwald Building, so named because it, like several others that had begun to dot Texas rural areas, was made possible by the Rosenwald Fund.

My enrollment consisted of children in grades one through five. Students above the fifth grade were transported by bus to the district high school.

The Lost Prairie community was less than twenty miles from Pine Hill, which I had left two years earlier, but I immediately discerned a difference in the two. At Lost Prairie I recognized a community solidarity and high aspirations that were absent at Pine Hill.

By now the Federal government had begun to reach into the isolated and deprived areas, and President Roosevelt's efforts to eradicate nutritional ills affecting one-third of the population were in high gear. Government commodities, with food service personnel paid with federal funds, obviated the need for hot-lunch improvisations such as I had employed in prior years. Our vacant room was used as a food preparation and dining room.

Following my usual mode of operation, I organized a PTA that remained active, but was not phenomenal in any way. Since there was a high school in the district, and all families were associated to some degree with its program, the small school's activities were relegated to a somewhat minor role.

In spite of the isolation and the supportive status of the Lost Prairie school, I enjoyed my work. The most oppressive feature of my years there had to do with transportation. I still did not own an automobile, and the idea of Frank providing the taxi service was immediately ruled out by our prior experience. Then, too, there was no second teacher to share the travel expenses. No matter what problems might arise, I was not about to sacrifice the sweet prospect of coming home at the end of each workday. So, encouraged by my lucrative salary, I decided to hire a commercial taxi outright.

Since I have always held a reverent regard for getting to work on time, my concern when the driver occasionally was late worsened. I dismissed three drivers before I found a young man who measured up to my standards of punctuality.

Finding a reliable driver with a dependable vehicle was only one component of my transportation problem, and by no means ended my trouble. One five-mile stretch of road, rugged at best, became almost impassable with even a light shower. Whenever nightfall was accompanied by a slow drizzle, I would develop a mild case of insomnia. If I awakened during the night to the rhythm of rain on the roof, my peaceful slumber was ended. I would spend the remainder of the night wondering how we would manage to get to work on time. I was acutely aware that the only way I could avoid being late on such days was by the grace of God supplementing my driver's skill. On numerous occasions the grace of God must have been in short supply, for there was one small depression in the clay road that a few inches of water would quickly transform into an axle-deep chuckhole. Our car became stuck in this bog so frequently that a kindly farmer who lived nearby placed several poles beside the road. The purpose, he explained, was to "help the teacher out of the bog."

In assessing my Lost Prairie situation with its various positive and negative factors, an acquaintance once remarked, "Happiness is Dorothy and a group of school kids." I think her assessment was valid.

The decision to move me to the high school was not mine, and in fact was made over my protest, but the basis for the decision was interesting.

Since the creation of the Texas Education Agency (TEA) in the late 1940s, the state office has maintained a relatively close association with local school people. The Education Service Centers made this kind of liaison possible, but this was not the story in the

1930s and early 1940s. A visit by a state department representative was an occasion of great consequence. If there was prior knowledge of the visit, as there generally was unless the local school was suspect in some area, special efforts were made to present the school in its most favorable light. Even in systems that prided themselves on honest accounting and "had nothing to hide," there was likely to be a modicum of "brushing up." Buildings and grounds were refurbished; lesson plans refined, and students enjoined to exhibit their best behavior. Such was the existing climate in early 1941 when William Herber Dailey, the principal of Flint Hill High School, informed me of the forthcoming visit of a state department official. I was told that, in addition to visiting the high school, he would visit Lost Prairie, since he was concerned with the total program of the district. Our destiny rested with this official since he would determine our eligibility for continued state aid. I can say with all honesty that I tried to develop and use meaningful lesson plans. My housekeeping was above average, so I felt no trepidation at the approaching visit. I followed the usual custom, however, and did "a little something extra."

Learning the approximate hour of the visit, I consulted my daily schedule and found that the visitor would probably arrive during the social studies period. We were engaged in a study unit on Hawaii, and it was in this setting that I planned our star performance.

I borrowed a portable record player (it was called a phonograph then) and procured a Hawaiian record. The crucial day proved to be the kind that every experienced teacher recognizes as a rarity. Everything moved according to schedule, and we had just begun our class activities when the principal and the state visitor entered the room.

Our Hawaiian record was being played and the room was filled with the lilting, fluid strains of a Hawaiian melody. Greetings were extended with some noticeable distraction on the part of the pupils. In order to regain their attention, I said, "You recall we've read about the beautiful tall palms that grow in Hawaii. As you listen to the record can't you just see the palm trees waving?" One forward youngster responded immediately by saying, "I don't see them, but I hear them." His forthright and realistic reaction evoked laughter from us all and set the tone for healthy class interaction that resulted in a pleasant experience. In departing, the visitor made some complimentary remarks about my teaching procedure. The principal beamed his pleasure and I ended my day, happy that the visit was now history and I could now move on to other concerns. Little did I dream what they would be.

A few days later, the principal again visited the Lost Prairie School. This was not unusual for, officially, I was under his general supervision. Yet, because he had full confidence in my ability and performance and a multitude of other responsibilities, he seldom came to the campus. Today he looked quite solemn and wasted no time in stating his purpose: "Dorothy, next year, I am going to move you to the high school. The state department representative told me that I was burying one of my strongest teachers here in a one-teacher school. You are a home economics major and it so happens that the present homemaking teacher will be leaving at the end of this school year. Moving you is the logical step to take." I did not agree then, nor do I agree now, that stronger teachers are needed in the high school than in the primary grades, but I was never one to resist authority. I did, however, express a desire to remain where I was. "I'm happy," I said, "out here among these pines with my little group."

Realizing the extent of the influence of the state official and the impact it would have on our application for state aid, the principal was inclined to regard any suggestion, or even any comment, from the visitor as tantamount to a directive. In view of this fact, my objections were fruitless. A few days later, I signed a contract to teach homemaking at Flint Hill High School for ten months at a salary of $127.50 per month. What a fabulous salary!

With this kind of financial assurance, there was one thing that I was certainly going to buy and that was freedom from my anxieties and frustrations of transportation. I could do nothing about road conditions, but I could at least own my own automobile. This goal was achieved on August 30, 1941, when I purchased my first car— a black, two-door Plymouth sedan. The contract called for thirty-six monthly payments of $27.50 each. I do not recall the down payment, but it was minimal.

The Redus family, 1910. My parents (Caleb and Susie Redus) with my brother George and me when I was ten months old.

With tenth-grade classmates at Yoakum High School. I'm the tall one on the right.

This picture was made of me during the 1929-30 school year. I had begun teaching in October, 1928. I wore my hair done up in the fashion
of the day with the stylish "question mark" dangling over my forehead.

Frank and I on the steps of the old veterinary hospital at Prairie View College, June, 1930, four weeks before we were married.

The Redus family, summer of 1939. My mother and father (Susie America and Caleb Isaiah) are seated. My three brothers are, left to right, Carlly Lee, Caleb Raleigh, and George Elzy. We three girls are, left to right, Loda Belle, Leona Harlene, and myself.

With my Markham school students, Matagorda County, May, 1933. Note the flag.

Above, Frank in his basement office in the Anderson County court-house, 1933. Below, Frank demonstrates land terracing techniques to black farmers, Anderson County, early 1930s.

Above, the County Council of Black Farmers meet at the Anderson County courthouse in 1933 to receive information on improved farming practices. Frank, front row, wearing boots, was among the speakers who participated. Below, the speakers included, left to right, R. P. Lee, M. E. Lyons, Frank, H. L. Price, and Hunter Barrett.

Above, one of the typical Anderson County canning kitchens, mid-1930s. Below, the Pine Hill school student body, 1934-35. I had sixty-three children enrolled in this rural, one-teacher school in Anderson County, nine miles from Palestine, Texas.

Above, a 4-H girl feeds her turkeys as part of the Live at Home program, 1937. Below, a countywide 4-H Club meeting at the Anderson County courthouse in 1937 under the supervision of Frank and the Extension Service, also part of the Live at Home program.

Above, demonstrating a peanut picker to the County Council of Black Farmers, Anderson County courthouse, late 1930s. Below, a butchering demonstration is given by the Extension Service in Anderson County, 1940. Note that every man wears a tie.

Above, parents take a break from clearing stumps from the Pine Hill school campus to sit for a portrait, 1934-35. Below, preschoolers look on as the menfolk clear stumps and the women prepare to serve lunch. Opposite above, mules were used to both pull stumps and level the ground. Opposite below, a group attacks a stump.

Mrs. Betty Ealy, treasurer of the Pine Hill school PTA, and her son, W. H., and granddaughter, 1934-35. Mrs. Ealy kept the PTA funds tied up in a handkerchief, often secreted in her bosom.

Right, my graduation portrait from Prairie View State College. I graduated in 1937 with honors, receiving a Bachelor of Science degree in home economics. Below, furniture being repaired in the Home Project Short Course, Flint Hill High School, December, 1941.

Above, Flint Hill High School faculty, early 1940s. The principal, William H. Dailey, is seated. I am directly behind him. Below, students participate in the scrap metal drive, Palestine, Texas, 1942.

On September 1, 1941, I drove upon Flint Hill campus as the new homemaking teacher. I had visited the campus on numerous occasions, but that day I looked at the plant with new eyes. I felt new challenges and envisioned new goals. Here indeed was an old bottle, for Flint Hill was the first rural high school for blacks in Anderson County. My responsibility, as I saw it, was to supply new wine.

Except for size, the Flint Hill plant was no improvement over the school buildings in the other district in which I had worked. There was the main building of six classrooms; a vocational building of four rooms, one of which served as a shop; a teacherage; and a kitchen and lunchroom built of logs. This structure also served as a canning kitchen and housed a grist mill.

There was no auditorium, no library, no gymnasium, no storage room, and no laboratory. There was not one piece of audio-visual equipment; yet this was an accredited high school.

Teachers were expected to live in the teacherage. By so doing, it was felt that they would become more involved in community affairs and thereby have a more positive impact upon community life. I suspect most teachers welcomed the privilege of living on the campus, for it eliminated the need to seek lodging in homes, most of which were already overcrowded. It also eliminated the possibility of bogging down on the muddy roads during the rainy season. But I had my new car, and I had no intention of letting muddy roads or the availability of a room in the teacherage interfere with my commuting the fifteen miles daily to school.

I assured the principal that neither distance nor weather would prevent my getting to work on time. I further supported my stand by reminding him that an effective homemaking teacher made home visits after school and some of the homes I would be visiting were nearer to my own home than to the school. My promise was fulfilled, for I generally arrived on the campus before the occupants of the teacherage, even though I sometimes had to park my car at a farmhouse and walk the last two or three miles.

In my long career as a teacher, I seldom saw a more capable and versatile staff than the group with whom I worked at Flint Hill, nor have I seen a staff more willing to give of itself. Each of the nine persons on the faculty carried extra responsibilities. For example, the coach taught history, and the manual-arts teacher doubled as a bus driver; one middle-grades teacher taught typing, another taught public school music and trained the high school choral group; and the principal taught mathematics. After so many years of working alone, I found unending motivation through daily contact with this group of young, energetic professionals.

For the first time in my teaching career, I really studied an official teacher's guide. I am not sure that I had ever seen one before. While the guide offered tremendous help, I found it ill-suited in many respects to my setting. It was developed with certain basic assumptions concerning facilities and equipment, much of which was completely lacking in my department. My inventory consisted of three Singer sewing machines, two of which were in need of repair, and a kitchen range. There also was an odd assortment of cooking utensils and serving pieces, too few in number to accommodate my enrollment of sixty girls. Furthermore, the homemaking department could claim no bedroom, no living room, and no furniture, yet the course of study prescribed by the state department assumed the presence of a laboratory setting that included these basic household components.

Except for adopted texts, I do not believe there was one book to serve as a homemaking library, and the library materials that I brought to the department were embarrassingly limited. Bulletins from the Extension Service office proved to be our main source of reference.

Once the total scope of our deprivation was determined, I set about arranging substitutes for some needs and convincing myself that we would have to operate without others, no matter what the state department prescribed.

I arranged with the occupants of the teacherage to use its living and dining rooms as a laboratory. Under my supervision, the homemaking students selected wallpaper and, with the aid of the coach who had some expertise in the hanging of paper, we papered the rooms. Students from the woodworking classes joined the homemaking girls in refinishing the floors and the chairs and tables, not one piece of which seemed compatible with another. The advanced girls made curtains for the windows. A few hooked and Singercraft

scatter rugs added the final touch. The end product was an acceptable facsimile of a dining and living room area.

Money for the operation of the foods laboratory was extremely
limited, but experience in menu planning, food selection and pur-
chasing, and food preparation and service was extended by assign-
ing girls on a rotating schedule to work with the hot-lunch program.
The school garden became the joint project of the homemaking girls
and the boys enrolled in vocational agriculture. Using such substi-
tution and compromise, we were able minimally to satisfy the state
guide.

We implemented a unit on "Worthy Use of Leisure Time," suggested in the guide, and culminated it with a hobby show involving
the whole community. There were displays of needlework, handicraft, hunting gear, and woodcraft. There were demonstrations in
game playing, gardening techniques, and sewing. There were even
several saddle horses to focus on horseback riding as a hobby.

A child-care unit was included in the state guide. To satisfy this
phase of our program, the students brought their preschool siblings,
cousins, nieces, and nephews to school, and thus provided a live
laboratory. This increased the passenger load of the buses and provided amusement for the regular bus riders. The bus drivers, on the
other hand, found nothing amusing about the presence of a group
of hyperactive, noisy preschoolers on their already overcrowded,
delapidated buses.

The clothing courses seem to have generated more sustained interest than any other homemaking units. This may be attributed
to an interest in wearing apparel that seems to be an innate feminine concern. Each unit in clothing was culminated with a style
show or fashion revue.

This was always an event of great moment. What enhances the
self-image more than an awareness of one's creative powers and the
recognition of those powers by others? An ancient philosopher
once proclaimed that the joy of creation is one of the ten great joys
of life. The truth of this statement was supported by the pride with
which those young girls displayed their simple creations. Stepping
to the piano rhythms provided by the music teacher, they paraded
before an appreciative audience showing a cotton print, a pique, or

an organdy garment made from material that ranged in price from twenty-five cents to ninety-eight cents per yard.

Pictures were always made for the homecoming scrapbook. The event ended with the girls feeling especially proud of themselves and the citizens of the community feeling that school indeed meant more than the three Rs. The teacher was always relieved at the termination of the project; she could now direct her energies to the next unit, that in most cases had already been lifted from the state guide and modified to meet local needs and adjusted to a situation characterized by improvisations.

That the Flint Hill homemaking program was successful is hardly debatable, but evaluators attempting to determine the reason for its success probably would find an area of disagreement. Was it the course content, the method of approach, or the impact of the teacher's personality? Was it a combination of these? There has been no formal follow-up of the girls who were my students at Flint Hill, but my personal observations have revealed some interesting facts.

I know of three who became homemaking teachers and one who entered the Extension Service as a home demonstration agent. One is a recreation supervisor, one a professional dressmaker, another a licensed vocational nurse. Sometimes I meet on the street a graying grandmother who says with pride, "Mrs. Robinson, I made this dress that I am wearing." Occasionally—as if to supply a retired teacher with reason to live—in pleasant retrospect she will add, "I also sew for my daughters and my grandchildren."

Some thirty years now separate me from my Flint Hill tenure, and a time slot of that magnitude should increase the objectivity and validity of any evaluative attempt on my part. Looking back, I still feel that the high school homemaking programs of that day were extremely helpful, but I am not sure that the greatest benefits were derived from the formal courses. Much of the learning was concomitant in nature. The extracurricular activities resulted in outcomes that rivaled the formal goals set up in the state homemaking guide.

Experiences that I gained through New Homemakers of Texas

(NHT) activities support my belief in this regard. Prior to school integration in Texas, black students enrolled in vocational home-making were not affiliated with the Future Homemakers of America (FHA). Instead, they were identified with a separate national organization whose official name was New Homemakers of America (NHA). As I recall, the NHA was in its formative stages when I was at Flint Hill. At one of the last professional homemaking meetings I attended, in 1944, we gave considerable consideration to Texas's role in the national organization. At that time the organization operating in Texas, to which my students belonged and for which I provided local sponsorship, was the NHT. This organization provided a comprehensive and appealing program of activities, the implementation of which was limited only by the ingenuity and commitment of those involved.

There were opportunities for the development of such needed attributes as leadership and followership ability, interest in civic affairs, a knowledge of parliamentary procedure, a respect for the democratic process, skill in news gathering and reporting, and an appreciation for innate talents.

Each year at the state NHT convention, a talent contest was staged, an apt designation of which could well have been, Mini Miss America Pageant. The oratory, the musical renditions, and the dance techniques exhibited on those occasions gave testimony to the natural endowments of the young students and forecasted future possibilities. Two young ladies who first marketed their wares at the NHT convention became professional entertainers. One became famous in Dallas, Houston, and other cities of the Southwest while the other gained national acclaim as a pianist and a singer. As schools become more institutionalized and less student oriented, focus on this type of individual development is reduced.

As I view school integration and study its impact on student life, I am inclined to believe that it is in the area of extracurricular activities that black students suffer most. This is not to say that there is widespread deliberate discrimination against minority students, but there is no denying that it exists and few indeed are the school officials and the school systems that have addressed themselves to the alleviation of this situation. Several factors contribute to the limited participation of black students in extracurricular activities.

Sometimes roles are filled by elections, and even the slightest inclination to vote along racial lines insures success for the dominant ethnic group. Many administrators and sponsors discourage leadership roles for blacks because they embrace the misconception that white students will not follow the leadership of blacks. Leadership is colorless, and this has been proved on numerous occasions when a broader view has prevailed. Black parents are inclined either to discourage or assume an apathetic attitude about their children participating in competitive endeavors because they frequently feel that the decisions may be biased. Because of many deprivations, either real or imagined, numbers of black students lack self-confidence and need special encouragement from teachers and counselors. All too often this special encouragement is woefully lacking.

In a culture characterized by rigid social barriers, many paradoxes exist. In our country, one of the most flagrant is our concern for the conservation of natural resources—land, forest, water, and wildlife—yet we carelessly exploit human potential. The minds of its citizens are this country's greatest resource, and able minds have been distributed throughout the land without regard for sex, economic status, geographical location, or ethnic derivation. I have embraced this concept since my youth, and my years at Flint Hill did much to support it.

7

BITTER BREAD

O NE OF THE MOST fascinating sides of home-
making education, and certainly one of the most profitable as it
related to the tax dollar, is that phase dealing with adult education.
It has been gratifying to note the modern trend toward many areas
of vocational training and retraining for adults, but in the 1940s,
especially in the small, rural communities, vocational offerings for
adults were generally limited to evening classes in agriculture and
homemaking.

So early in my Flint Hill tenure, I organized an evening class for
adult homemakers. This was certainly not innovative and I can lay
no claim to originating the idea. It was simply the thing to do and
every effective homemaking teacher conducted evening classes as a
part of her total homemaking program. The evening classes made
it possible for housewives to upgrade their homemaking skills.
Moreover, the practice of involving mothers and daughters together
in areas of common interest did much to strengthen family unity.

Just as the high school students chose and worked on home projects, so did the mothers. If a project was very elaborate, a cooperative approach was sometimes used. Having developed both skill
and confidence from our work at refurbishing the teacherage, we
became engaged in some rather ambitious projects. Sometimes I
would take a group of girls to a home where we would work with
the housewife in papering a room or in refinishing a suite of furniture.

Demands for this kind of cooperation became so great that some adjustments had to be made. In my frantic search for a solution, I devised a plan that I can still claim as my own. Borrowing the term "short course" from the Extension Service people, and aiming to work on home projects, I organized an effort called Home Project Short Course. I had never heard of one before, nor have I heard of one since. Anyway, this venture proved to be as successful as it was unique.

A two-week period was designated for the activity. Everyone in the community who had a project, any part of which was exportable, was invited to participate. The morning of the first day found the campus cluttered with wagons, trucks, and automobiles. Long lines of men and women registered in the main room of the vocational building. There was no registration fee. The only cost involved was for materials. Such tools and equipment as the school owned were at the disposal of the participants.

When the work really got underway, the men and boys repaired farm implements and stoves and made such items as gates, hog troughs, and yard furniture. The women and girls made draperies; reupholstered chairs and sofas; refinished and painted beds, tables, and chairs; made rugs and mattresses; pieced quilts; and mended leaky cooking utensils. It is highly probable that everyone who participated in that short course remembers it as one of the busiest periods of his life, for it was ten days of frantic activity. The event was culminated with a giant exhibit. The county superintendent, the trustees, and officials from the state department were invited as special guests.

Having to operate without the covenience of the instant camera, weeks passed before we could display our "before and after" pictures but, when they were posted in the main hallway, they told a graphic story of what a little money and a lot of hard work can accomplish. But even the pictures could not portray the self-esteem that the families felt in living in improved surroundings.

I firmly adhere to the belief that the success of any undertaking is determined primarily by the quality of the planning that precedes its initiation. As the time for the Home Project Short Course neared in early December, 1941, I intensified my efforts to disseminate information about the event. I wanted every family in the district to have a very thorough understanding of what was being planned, and how the total operation would be conducted. There was no television. Some homes were without radios, and many families had no children in school. Then too, the Flint Hill District was comprised of three distinct communities. So the problem of reaching every family became, at least in part, a matter of personal contact. To simplify this chore, I decided to visit the churches in each community on "pastorial day" and utilize a few minutes during the worship service to advertise the forthcoming event. Sunday, December 7, 1971, found me thus engaged.

The services at the Flint Hill Baptist Church were lengthy in keeping with the usual practice of most rural churches of that day. Also, my remarks added something to the length of our stay that morning. Even after adjournment, I lingered a while on the grounds to answer a few direct questions and to add a word of encouragement to a few citizens who appeared ambivalent about their decision to participate in the short course. Finally, physical fatigue or a rational feeling that I had accomplished all that I could reasonably expect dictated that I end my mission. So I left the church, satisfied and at peace with the world. I finally arrived home about mid-afternoon.

The moment I entered the house, Frank and my sister Leona, who was visiting in our home, cried out in unison, "The Japs have bombed Pearl Harbor." To be honest, I did not know where Pearl Harbor was and I am not sure I had ever heard of it before. Certainly I had no inkling of the full import of their statement. But before I retired that night, my knowledge of geography, history, international relations, and political strategy was considerably increased because we huddled around the radio for the remainder of the day listening to descriptions of the attack, and to reports of the reaction of President Roosevelt and other high officials of state.

It was a somber group of teachers who arrived on the Flint Hill campus on Monday morning, December 8, 1941. I suppose we were all in a state of shock, for we must have had some concept of the gravity of the situation, but the awesomeness of the total impact upon our individual lives and upon us as a group could not yet be known.

We lifted the hinged partition that separated two rooms in the main building, thus converting them into a sort of auditorium. The students filed in quietly and seated themselves in a very orderly manner until all seats were taken. Others stood in the aisles along the walls. This was regular procedure as there were never enough seats to accommodate the whole student body. The entire faculty and student body were finally assembled and listened to the radio address by President Roosevelt in which he declared: "Yesterday, December 7, 1941—a date which will live in infamy—the United States of America was suddenly and deliberately attacked by naval and air forces of the Empire of Japan." He continued by outlining steps America would take in retaliation to Japan's acts of aggression.

Even in times of stress, Franklin D. Roosevelt's voice had a comforting and assuring quality. So at the end of the speech, even the children in that remote rural school in deep East Texas felt something of the urgency and challenge of the time—a feeling that was to grow and intensify during the next three and one-half years.

The changes that took place in America after the declaration of war were swift and decisive. A new seriousness developed among our students. A new interest in current events was born. Expression and acts of patriotism were commonplace, but then that was when praying in school was not a violation of the law and teachers felt that a discussion of moral issues was still within the purview of their responsibilities to students.

A call was sent out for scrap metal. Our principal organized our school in a metal-salvaging contest, giving special recognition to the rooms and to the individuals that brought the largest amount of scrap metal to school on certain days.

Daylight Saving Time was declared. The rationale for this act was that by beginning the school day earlier, the school day would end earlier and the students would then have more time to engage in farm labor and other types of employment. There was an immediate increased need for young people in the labor market, for within the matter of a few months, the absence of men in the community was noticeable. Any protest about Daylight Saving Time could be described as a mild complaint, although I did find it strange to drive to school during winter mornings with my car lights brightly beaming.

The school garden was enlarged and the vegetables produced were canned under my supervision for the next year's hot-lunch supply. A defense class was organized on our campus, the purpose of which was to instruct farmers in the repair of their own machinery and tools thereby saving money and extending the life of their farm equipment. A local mechanic served as instructor for courses offered in this class.

Temporary offices for the issuance of ration books were set up at various points in the county. I worked as a member of the team that staffed the office in the Flint Hill community. The rationing of meat, sugar, and gasoline seemed to have resulted in greater inconvenience for the average family than did the rationing of many other items.

Along with other home economists, I geared my program to the war effort. I immediately revamped the course plans for my students. The renovation and coordination of clothing received great emphasis. Recipes were collected and demonstrations and lectures were given on the use of meat substitutes, honey, and artificial sweetners. Food production and preservation received new national emphasis. A popular slogan of that time was, "Food will win the war and write the peace." The members of my adult class organized a Victory Garden Contest. Variety, quality, and quantity of vegetables were factors considered by the judging team that was composed of other homemaking teachers of the country. Of course due recognition was given to the winners.

To further emphasize the importance of food production, community meat shows were held under the auspices of local extension agents. This idea was expanded by district extension agents and finally district meat shows were held with several counties entering on a competitive basis. For three successive years, Anderson County won first place under Frank's supervision.

The phase of homemaking that I liked least was the canning of food but, as I entered into this distasteful work, I tried to keep my disdain concealed. Wasn't the country at war? Wasn't everyone supposed to make a sacrifice? Flint Hill was more fortunate than

most communities. Even before the war the agriculture club, working with the Extension Service program under supervision of Frank
and the home demonstration agent (Mrs. Irene S. Kinchion), had
constructed a community canning kitchen. As produce from the
various victory gardens was harvested, it was often brought to this
canning kitchen. There, during the hot summers of 1942 and 1943,
I toiled and perspired with farm families. We canned peas, beets,
carrots, beans, onions, sauerkraut, tomatoes, okra, peaches, berries,
and pears. Beeves were butchered and chili, stews, steaks, and roasts
were canned.

The ancient method of preserving food by drying was revived.
Although I disliked this method of preservation less than canning,
we did not engage in it very extensively. I think my greatest accomplishment was in the oven-drying of peaches, but I doubt that
the end product would have won a ribbon at the county fair.

My course in family relationship was modified, for the war made
new demands on family members. Many decisions and adjustments
had to be made, and these often had to be made under stress with
little time for discussion and sound thinking.

One day one of my senior girls told me that her boy friend, who
was also a senior, had enlisted in the army. She wondered if they
should get married before he left or if they should wait until his
return. Who was I to offer advice on a subject so vital, in a time so
uncertain? I frankly admitted my inadequacy, but promised to use
her dilemma as a class problem. The problem was offered in the
abstract and the girls in the class were asked to list reasons why the
couple should marry before the young man left and to list reasons
why the marriage should be delayed. As might be expected, this
exercise evoked a lively response.

I never knew if this influenced the young couple's decision, but
they did get married before his departure. He died in the Port Chicago explosion near Pittsburg, California, in 1944, leaving a pregnant wife. The child of that union is now a public school teacher
in San Antonio, Texas.

We felt from the beginning that we were making our contribution
to the war effort, and we were. But our efforts were more or less
indirect. We suffered—or rather we experienced—the inconvenience

of rationed food, long workdays, and the shortage of nylon hose and household linens. We were engaged in the war somewhat vicariously, because it was the others who were submitting to the rigors of basic training, manning the guns, suffering the combat injuries, and winning the Purple Hearts. No one from our community had become a war casualty yet. There was a sort of glamour about the letters and trinkets sent to relatives and sweethearts by soldiers from faraway places with strange-sounding names.

During the 1942-43 school year, we were drawn more directly into the war. Our agriculture teacher was inducted. This was a blow to the morale of the whole vocational department. Although he was replaced by a capable older man, the vocational agriculture classes—and the homemaking classes for that matter—never seemed the same. A short time later one of our young teachers resigned to take a clerical position in Washington, D.C., where she still resides. This was the beginning of the end of our strong faculty.

By September, 1943, the principal had resigned to take a defense job in Los Angeles. His wife, one of the primary teachers, accompanied him. The music teacher joined her husband who had entered the military service; the English teacher had gotten married and had moved to the West Coast. So the school year began at Flint Hill with an almost new faculty.

In the hiring of personnel that year, the Flint Hill school board was faced with a problem that was to become more acute as the war progressed, and was to remain extant for some time after the cessation of hostilities. That problem had to do with the recruitment of capable administrators and teachers. For then, as now, certification was not synonymous with qualification.

Try as hard as I might, I could not recoup the spirit and the motivation of the old Flint Hill. I worked hard but the zest and fulfillment were gone. I suppose I would have remained however, had not Frank resigned his position with the Extension Service effective January 1, 1944.

For years he had suffered severely from a respiratory disorder that was aggravated each summer by dust and pollen. His doctor had recommended a change of climate. Defense workers were needed on the West Coast, so this seemed like the logical time to change climates. Frank left for San Francisco, California, on January 5, 1944. Some two months later, at the end of the first semester, I left Flint Hill, never to enter a classroom again to teach high school homemaking.

8

THE CAMELOT YEARS

$\mathcal{A}$T 11:40 A.M. on September 14, 1947, we entered Texas, crossing the state line near Texarkana. Our three and one-half year stay in San Francisco was now history. Although San Francisco is a romantic, historical city and possesses much natural beauty, I had never enjoyed living there. I detested the fog, the wind, and the attached houses. I have visited major cities on five continents, and except for Paris and Rio de Janeiro, I know of none that rival San Francisco for sheer color and individuality. But these attributes did little to increase my affection for my temporary home. It was with profound joy that I departed from the Golden Gate city.

Had we chosen the most direct route for our motor trip home, we would have entered Texas on the western boundary, but to satisfy our yen for travel, we elected to follow a more circuitous route and drove leisurely through the states of Nevada, Utah, Wyoming, Colorado, Kansas, and Arkansas. We brought back with us memories both pleasant and unpleasant of our California stay.

In the happy category we could list the lucrative salaries we both had earned. We had cleared the mortgage on our house and for the first time in our married life we had established a meager savings account. We had some educational and cultural experiences that never could have been ours had we stayed in Anderson County, Texas. Frank had taken advanced courses in blueprint reading and carpentry, and I had studied bookkeeping and interior decoration. I discovered San Francisco State Teachers College from which I was later to receive the master's degree. We watched the launching of a major battleship and stood amid the vast cheering crowd that welcomed General Jonathan Wainwright of Bataan and Corregidor fame as he paraded triumphantly through the streets of San Francisco after being held for thirty-nine months in Japanese prison camps. I had broken the color barrier to become the first black woman to serve on the dietetic staff of San Francisco City and County Hospital. We had attended stage plays and had seen in person many of the popular entertainers of that era including Bing Crosby, Frank Sinatra, Lena Horne, Jimmie Lunceford, Count Basie, Louis Armstrong, Dinah Shore, Duke Ellington, Lionel Hampton, and Nat King Cole. Most gratifying of all, Frank's health was much improved.

The sudden death of my mother on November 18, 1944, heads the list of unpleasant memories. In the late afternoon of that date, I received a telegram telling me that she was stricken. Some six hours later a second message informed me that she was gone.

I think I was more shocked than saddened. Mama had been preparing me for her death since my early childhood. She frequently punctuated her motherly advice and simple homilies with the statement, "Mama won't be with you always." So I was constantly reminded of the sureness of her death. But when the reference became a fact, I found it difficult to accept the truth that within a time span of six hours I could be robbed of the living presence of this quiet, little woman who spent her sixty-five years in a shy, unassuming, self-effacing manner that concealed from many who were close to her, the depth of her thinking, the strength of her character, her sensitivity to beauty, and the extent of her dreams. Once in a pensive mood, my sister asked me if I thought I would ever see our mother again. I replied, "I don't know. Whether I see her again is not important. To have known her and to have been influenced by her is enough for me, for surely she left her spirit with me." And that she surely did.

Upon receiving the message telling me of mama's plight, I began preparations to return to Texas. Getting from San Francisco, California, to Bay City, Texas, was no simple matter in November,

1944. Because of urgent wartime measures, major airlines gave priority to service personnel. Reservations for civilian passengers were subject to instantaneous cancellation. In view of this practice, Frank and I decided that I should return to Texas by train. It was on this trip aboard the Sunset Limited of the Southern Pacific Lines that I encountered the most humiliating and flagrant act of racial discrimination I have ever known.

White prisoners-of-war (Germans I suppose) were marched under guard through my coach to enjoy a meal in the dining car to which I had been denied admittance. On that day, while the train stood at the station of a small town, I munched on a dry sandwich purchased from a street vendor, and wondered how Americans, especially black Americans, could sing of the "land of the free." I cursed the democracy that would demand the supreme sacrifice of my brothers who were then on active duty, and deny me the privilege of eating a meal simply because I was black.

I had further reason to recognize the sheer hypocrisy of American democracy because of an incident that occurred about two years later. The hypocrisy was all the more brazen because of California's claims of freedom from ethnic biases. Frank, my sister and her husband (Leona and Claude Sansom), and I decided to spend Christmas at a mountain retreat called Pine Crest. I made arrangements for a cabin through a downtown travel agency. We made the trip and were received with nothing more formidable than a few stares of curiosity. When our three-day stay ended, we made special effort to leave our cabin in impeccable condition. We justified our extra efforts by reminding each other that since we were the only black guests at the retreat, our quarters would probably be subjected to severe scrutiny and we did not want to do anything that would support the myth that black people are dirty and disorderly.

Imagine my chagrin when a few days after returning to the city, I received a telephone call from the travel agency and a horrified voice announced, "Mrs. Robinson, we hear that you had Negroes in your party at Pine Crest at Christmas." I answered with a voice that I hoped portrayed my utter disgust, "We were *all* Negroes. Now what is wrong with that? I made our reservations in person and I made no effort to conceal my racial identity, and you expressed no interest in that regard." The shock at the other end was expressed with heavy silence. I followed the telephone conversation with a letter that generated an acceptable apology from the travel agency and a written invitation from the management at Pine Crest inviting us to return at any time. Naturally, that is one invitation we have never honored.

Although both the pleasant and the unpleasant memories of our stay in San Francisco are still indelibly etched in my consciousness, in September, 1947, my joy of being at home served to minimize their importance. The romance of San Francisco's fog, the enchantment of its attached houses, the lure of its bridges, the grandeur of its peaks, and the exotic sounds and glitter of its Chinatown could not compare with the drab clay hills and the lordly green pines of East Texas. If I were ever truly an individual, this must have been the time, for perhaps no other person in the whole world would have preferred the latter. I devoted the last quarter of 1947 to redecorating our house. The new year found me with leisure time to use as I pleased. This was the first time since I began school at the age of eight that winter months found me disengaged, and I soon learned that it was not a happy state for me.

I was determined to get back in the classroom the next fall, so I began early to make my desires known. By the end of April I had signed a contract to teach homemaking in a rural high school in a nearby county.

This contract was never honored, for in midsummer, Paul Rutledge, a classmate of mine and principal of the Green Bay High School, invited me to join his staff. He declared that he was in agreement with the county superintendent who had said, "We should not lose Dorothy Robinson to another county as badly as we need strong teachers here in Anderson County." So September, 1948, found me back in the classroom where I was destined to remain until my retirement.

I do not recall my exact salary, but two years later I was earning an annual salary of $2,655. For this magnificent sum I thanked the Minimum Foundation Program. My good fortune was almost incredible. I could hardly conceive of earning that kind of money for doing a job that I enjoyed so much; I would have done it without any compensation had my economic status made this possible.

At Green Bay I was again to know the enthusiasm that could be generated by daily association with capable, dedicated, ingenious teachers. My assignment was to teach the sixth grade, but because of the unity of the staff and the close articulation between all staff members, each teacher on the faculty was a resource person for me. I in turn reciprocated and lent my assistance to the others, especially to the homemaking teacher, the speech teacher, and the debate coach.

Like the Flint Hill High School, except for a strong faculty, Green Bay High School could lay positive claim to little else. The plant consisted of four separate buildings. The main building that consisted of six classrooms and a storage room was an architectural monstrosity that was the result of many makeshift additions. Another building consisted of one classroom and the principal's office. It had little to offer in the way of utility and nothing to offer in the way of beauty. The school kitchen and the lunchroom were housed in a third building that was equally lacking in appeal. The fourth and newest building on the campus was known as the vocational building because it housed the vocational agriculture and the homemaking departments. The vocational teachers were a husband and wife team, W. L. and Laurelia Singletary, who were generally recognized throughout the state for their superb leadership in their respective fields.

Again, improvisations were necessary. I used apple crates to make a bookcase for my classroom and later, when I was assigned the seventh grade also and my enrollment reached forty-six, I placed crude benches from the agriculture shop in the aisles so that every child would at least have a place to sit. Work areas were out of the question.

One of our improvisations became a tradition and a thing of beauty. That was the outdoor presentation of our annual operetta. Little did the vast audiences who enjoyed our performances know that the veritable fairyland that we contrived with lanterns and bowers of spring foliage was born of desperation. There was a total absence of adequate auditorium space.

It was in the presentation of the operetta that the unity of the faculty was poignantly expressed. The agriculture department and the physical education department had charge of building the temporary stage. The art department was responsible for the general properties. The homemaking students made the needed costumes. The music teacher directed the music; the English teacher directed the speaking parts; and the drama teacher coached the students in acting. Efforts were made to include all elementary students, even if it meant adding scenes or characters. The event gained such popularity that people from surrounding counties made annual visits to Green Bay to witness the operetta.

I was at Green Bay six years before the school had a gymnasium, but even in the absence of this facility the basketball team won the state championship on two occasions. I worked with the English teacher in coaching the debate team, and we won six state championships during my seven-year tenure. Winning music awards was standard procedure. The music teacher, Mrs. Johnnie Cephas Rutledge (the wife of the principal), was extremely competent and worked with piano students, the school choir, and small specialty groups. Each year our school won music awards in the Interscholastic League and, more often than not, the feat was repeated in agriculture and homemaking contests.

On several occasions Green Bay students represented Texas in regional and national contests. One Green Bay student, June Singletary, served one term as secretary of the NHA.

With so much emphasis on extracurricular activities, it might be assumed that these were given priority, but this was not the case. The basic three Rs were fundamental in the school's offerings. Excellent handwriting was, for many years, the hallmark of Green Bay students. Even today, it is not unusual for the quality of handwriting of former Green Bay students to elicit complimentary remarks.

With the exception of two or three severely retarded children, every student at Green Bay could read. This is not to say that all were excellent readers, or that all could read with equal competence, but each child could functionally interpret printed material on his level. To make this broad claim about a group of some 240 students ranging in grades from one to twelve is a strange gospel, at a time when remedial reading programs have become an integral part of the formal curricula of the nation's schools and millions of dollars are spent annually on remedial reading programs. The reverent homage that is paid to the present popular Right to Read programs almost leads one to think of the ability to read as a sacred gift reserved for the privileged few. In reality, any child who is free from major physical, emotional, and mental handicaps can be taught to read, and this feat can be accomplished by any teacher of average intelligence with average training who is willing to dedicate her efforts to this end.

The Green Bay faculty recognized the importance of professional growth and regarded it as a necessary continuing experience. Long before in-service days were mandated by state regulations, we were engaged in that type of activity. One of our major in-service projects was concerned with upgrading competences in the teaching of reading. The project grew to such proportions that it finally involved every school in the county, the county and district superintendents, and consultants from a nearby teacher-training institution. A report of the project was compiled in booklet form, and was used rather widely throughout the state as a reference by teachers of reading.

Before ADA (average daily attendance) became such a crucial factor in school financing, attendance at Green Bay was probably above the state average for similar rural schools, because teachers and parents set this as a joint priority.

Were it not for its serious implications, the issue of busing would be ludicrous to me. Like many other schools in Texas, Green Bay High School was a product of the consolidation era. Several small districts were combined. While this provided an enrollment sufficiently large to make the organization of a high school possible, it created the need for bus transportation. The same conditions maintained at the high school for whites. Sometimes white students were picked up literally at the door of the black school and bused to their school. The reverse was also true. It was a common sight to see two half-empty school buses moving almost bumper to bump-

er along U.S. Highway 79. Sometimes as few as six children comprised the passenger load, yet no one complained about the financial
waste of such an arrangement. And no one thought of integrating
the black and white passengers. Indeed, if the thought ever occurred, who was foolish enough or courageous enough to speak his
thoughts? Why such tumult about busing to achieve racial balance
when for years busing was maintained to perpetuate racial segregation?

When I view the strife, unrest, discord, and crime that is a great
part of today's campus scene, I have to struggle with my memory
to recall the Camelot years. But there really was a time when the
teacher-student relationship was one of mutual respect; when there
was a common understanding of the purpose of school, and a clear
delineation of the roles of teachers and students in achieving this
purpose. There really was a time when "teaching the whole child"
included efforts toward character building and value assessment.
There really was a time when teachers felt responsible for the moral
influence they exerted over their students and students felt that
teachers were worthy models. There really was such a time, and I
experienced it during my Green Bay years.

Thinking back over the many years that I taught and of the many
schools in which I worked, I never knew a school that encountered
fewer disciplinary problems than did Green Bay. I am still not sure
how this climate was achieved, for I found it in existence when I
joined the faculty; but I think it had its roots in strong, fair, consis-
tent, honest, careful administration. Paul Rutledge was a man of
deliberate cautious disposition. He hired his teachers with great
selectivity and then he proceeded to mold a school philosophy that
provided for diversity of thought, but a oneness of purpose. He
was not a flamboyant public relations man, but he created and
maintained a public awareness of what the school was doing and
he let the end product sell the program.

The type of discipline that was practiced at the Green Bay school
would be viewed with disfavor by the modern permissivist who feels
that imposed discipline thwarts the personality and frustrates the
individual. A follow-up of the Green Bay students with whom I

worked would give little support to this thesis. It is true that some five or six cannot be classified as law-abiding citizens, but the success stories are too numerous to be incidental. Without any special effort at research involving the current occupations of these former students, I can think of two high school principals, two pharmacists, one editor of a national magazine, one pharmaceutical salesman, one band director, a labor executive, a college professor, and six nurses, three of whom are employed at the same hospital in Houston, Texas. Also, one industrial manager, a television technician, and several teachers, most of whom are in the field of homemaking, two high-ranking military officers, two ministers, and several industrial workers.

I regard my Green Bay years as a period when my professional insights were strengthened. It was then that I began to think and act less as an individual teacher and more as a member of a team, a component of a system. This does not mean that I lost my identity and my individualism, Rather, I began to see that my worth as a teacher was enhanced when I functioned in relation to other teachers. I had never been uncooperative, but my early years of working alone had left its imprint upon my mode of operation.

The high esteem with which Green Bay High School was regarded and the broad, favorable recognition it enjoyed were based on a program geared to meet human needs. The needs of the people were always the first priority, and involving the whole community in the process of meeting those needs was the basic goal of the school. The strategy was to reach out to the people and not reach down to them.

Geographical location, inadequate financing, low socioeconomic level, lack of formal education, limited equipment, and the many other negative factors that influenced the way of life in the Green Bay community were never accepted as reasons or excuses for inferior performance on the part of teachers. There was absolutely no compromise on this score. While Paul Rutledge was fully aware of the advantages of an ideal school setting, he contended that the only two indispensable ingredients of a school were the teacher and the student. One of his favorite expressions was, "Teaching is but teaching whether it is done at Harvard, Green Bay, or Timbuktu."

By sheer exposure to this kind of thinking, the community gradually improved its self-image, and by the time I joined the school faculty the people felt something of a personal obligation to lift themselves.

Howard Thurman, former dean of the chapel at Boston University, and at one time listed as one of the ten most powerful preachers in America, says that his motto for dealing with people is, "Meet every man where he is, and treat him as you would if he were where he should be." Most of us at Green Bay never heard this expression, but in essence we practiced it and we all grew in the process. It was a happy cycle, with students, parents, and teachers gaining in luster and esteem because each lived to some extent in the reflected glory of the other. For seven years I enjoyed that glory, that esteem, and that growth.

9

THE LEAST OF THESE

*A*s HAPPY AS I was at Green Bay, there were
practical considerations with which I had to cope. Our enrollment,
which was never large, had peaked. Families had begun to leave the
farms and move into Palestine for such employment as they could
find. This meant an increase in enrollment in the Palestine Independent School District and a decrease in outlying districts, ours
included. If this trend continued, I could see a demand for additional teachers in Palestine and a possible reduction of staff at
Green Bay. I had no reason to think that I would be eliminated;
neither had I reason to think I would not. Why borrow trouble?

A second practical consideration was one of distance. Green
Bay, with a campus adjacent to U.S. Highway 79 about eight miles
from town, was one of the most accessible rural schools in Anderson County, but an assignment anywhere in the Palestine district
would be nearer my home. Frank and I had often discussed this.

Some years earlier, I had made formal application for employment in the Palestine district. My dossier consisted of an array of
testimonial letters and references. In a personal interview with one
of the board members, I was asked, "What is the least you will work
for?" I replied, "The state minimum." He responded, "Some people are willing to work for less in order to be at home." I assured
him that I was not one of those. Then he said that I was overqualified. Overqualified with only a baccalaureate degree and fourteen
years' experience! When the board met that year for hiring, it
employed a teacher whose paper qualifications were exactly the

same as mine—a baccalaureate degree and fourteen years' experience. When I mentioned this action to Frank, he very realistically reminded me that he had not been in position to do personal menial favors for the board member as had the spouse of the other applicant.

Once in an interview with the superintendent, he tapped lightly on my folder and said, "This is a good application, but I have several others equally good from which I can choose." I am sure he had several others, but I still wonder how closely several compared to mine. I thought of my years of residence in the Palestine school district, the amount of taxes we paid, my reputation as a teacher, my professional training, my teaching experience, and my involvement in community affairs; and I decided that the superintendent could not possibly regard me as a poor choice. Evidently, then, there were other applicants who were in better bargaining positions than I, and I thought I knew very well the nature of their bargains.

Suddenly the role in which I saw myself became repulsive to me. Why should I sit there and literally bargain with this man for an opportunity for employment? I gave voice to my innermost feelings: "I understand that my chances of ever being hired in Palestine are somewhat limited for, unfortunately, my mother never worked for any of the good white people here." With that the interview ended and so, I thought, did any possibility of my ever being elected to a position in the Palestine schools. When I reported the results of the interview to Frank, he said, "Did you really tell the superintendent that? He will never hire you now." I told him that I did not think the statement would affect my chances one way of the other, as apparently they had always been zero. But the scene changed.

One afternoon in late May, 1955, my telephone rang. After identifying himself, the Palestine superintendent told me that he had been aware for some time of the quality of work I had been doing and he wondered if I would be interested in a position in a special education program scheduled to begin the following September. His call actually followed conversation I had had with a member of the board in which upcoming vacancies were discussed. When a position in the high school mathematics department was mentioned, I admitted my weakness in that field and refused to consider the post. I likewise refused to consider a position as first grade teacher with the words, "As a first grade teacher, I am afraid I would not know what I was doing." Then I was told of the classes for mentally retarded and physically handicapped children that would be offered for the first time to blacks the following school year, and I was asked if I were interested in that. To this day, I cannot explain why I said yes.

It is true I had certification for teaching mentally retarded children, but the courses I had taken leading to that certification were purely incidental as far as I was concerned. I simply pursued them because my graduate adviser placed them on my program when I expressed no preference of electives. I certainly had no intention of ever teaching mentally retarded children. To a coworker who often expressed a desire to work with the mentally retarded, I had said repeatedly, "I want no part of it."

Perhaps, deep inside, I entertained a feeling of inadequacy, for I realized that special understanding, patience, tolerance, strength, and acceptance were necessary to work effectively with what one educational writer has referred to as "half a child." I must have felt that I did not possess the special qualities.

I still suffered from the feeling of helplessness I had experienced on my first day in a survey course dealing with education of the handicapped. On this occasion I was reduced to tears simply by watching a deaf child and a partially sighted child as they strove to cope with an environment designed primarily to accommodate a seeing and a hearing world. I was so disturbed I asked my adviser's permission to withdraw from the class, declaring that I was not emotionally fit to work with handicapped children. Her response was the most profound advice I ever received on working with handicapped children. For me it became a classic axiom, and I have passed it on numerous times to beginning teachers in the field of special education. She said, "Go back and see a *child*. See a child first with all of the basic needs of any child. Only after you have done that should you assess the child's difference." Throughout my many years of working in the field of special education, that statement served as a guiding principle. I do not think, however, that anything remotely connected with my professional training generated the affirmative answer to that school board member. It was as though a being outside of me made the response while I stood in silent approval. Afterward, a negative reply to the superintendent would have been contradictory. So again I said, "Yes." I signed the contract.

A second teacher employed to serve on the special education staff was Mrs. Helen Starr Hooper, a former student of mine from the Flint Hill years. A home economics graduate from Prairie View College, she had spent her earlier professional years as a county home demonstration agent. A very versatile, capable young woman, Helen was and still is a great dreamer with an unusual, cooperative optimistic disposition. Each of us was delighted to be associated with the other, but we had no notion who would supervise our program. We were enlightened on that matter when the superintendent called us in for a conference. After the conference ended, as we were departing from his office, he said, "Mrs. Robinson, since you have many years of experience, we shall depend on you to provide leadership for this program and to serve as principal of your building." It was thus that I was inducted into the awesome ranks of school administration and became at the same time both school principal and coordinator of special education.

When Helen accepted her position, it was understood that she would attend summer school to qualify for certification in her newly chosen field. In view of the rather lackadaisical manner in which I had pursued my first special education courses, I decided that, even though my grades were excellent and my credentials were intact, I should take additional courses with more serious intent. We both entered the University of Texas at Austin in early June. Helen's emphasis was in the field of the physically handicapped, mine in mental retardation.

Two weeks after registering at the university, while home for a weekend, I stepped awkwardly off my porch and fractured my ankle. Outfitted with a cast and crutches that I had considerable difficulty in learning to use, I returned to Austin feeling that I was a great burden to Helen. She did much to erase this feeling and combined her ministrations with those of my nephew, Willie C.

Alton, Jr., and Catherine M. Menter, who was to become his wife. Together they provided me with taxi service to the campus. By special permission, one of them drove my car to the entrance of the building where my classes were held. There I would hobble laboriously up the steps. The whole procedure was more inconvenient than painful. This trio brought me books from the library, and brought my meals to my room. I spent my hours of confinement reading, and most of the material I read pertained to the courses I was studying. So the *A* grade that I received in each course was due more to imposed restraints than to scholarship. My misfortune had generated a blessing.

After our summer of study, we both felt that we at least had enough knowledge to initiate and operate a special education program without making too many fatal errors. So then it was with considerable courage and optimism that we opened the doors of the Fourth Ward school at the beginning of the 1955-56 school year. Incidentally, the building had at one time served as a white elementary school. Its name then was Reagan Street School, but when it was opened to blacks, after being unoccupied for about five years, it was deemed expedient to change the name to that of the voting precinct.

Our building was a four-room, two-story brick structure. The rooms were large with high ceilings and each had an adjoining cloak and storage room. Windows occupied much of the wall space, providing a light, airy atmosphere. Two restrooms that were attached at the back of the ground floor gave evidence of having been added sometime after the original structure was completed. The halls were spacious and an angular staircase connected the two floors. There was no fire escape and, throughout the years we were housed in that building, I tried not to think of the grave peril we would face in the event of a fire.

When the building was constructed at the turn of the century, it was located in a lower middle-class white residential neighborhood. When we moved in, the neighborhood was in ethnic transition and the building was in need of some repair and redecoration. Some efforts at refurbishing had been made on the lower floor. Bats, spiders, and a few mice were left more or less undisturbed to share the dusty domain of the upper story.

Our enrollment that first year averaged about twenty-five students of which 60 percent were classified as mentally retarded, 40 percent as physically handicapped. In planning our schedule of work, it was decided to combine the two groups for clothing, woodworking, and foods. Helen would teach woodworking to the boys and clothing to the girls, and I would offer a course in foods for both boys and girls.

A section of Helen's room was designated as the woodworking shop and was outfitted with appropriate work benches and tools. In another section, she set up a sewing area, using old-fashioned treadle sewing machines, because the physical effort necessary to operate the machines was good therapy for some of the orthopedic children and did no harm to the others.

One side of my room was partitioned off for use as a kitchen. A work counter equipped with a sink was constructed. A new gas range and an electric refrigerator completed our basic kitchen needs. Contrary to what might have been expected, this department became as popular with the boys as with the girls, and several of the boys later entered the food-preparation field as adults.

One of the orthopedic boys in my first food class has had charge of the salad bar in a leading Dallas hotel for several years. Some of the boys indicated an interest in studying clothing and they were permitted to do so. The quality of workmanship that entered into some of the shirts and jackets they made rivaled that found in the garments the girls made.

Internally we were off to a good start, but externally there were problems. I do not think we were ever able to rate them according to seriousness, but we certainly had no difficulty in identifying a multitude. Most of our problems had their roots in lack of understanding of handicapping conditions and in misconceptions about the purpose of a special education program.

Many people, both lay persons and professionals, thought of mentally retarded children as being crazy and often referred to them as such. There were those who thought that mental retardation was contagious. A principal once said to me, "Mrs. Robinson, if you continue to work with these children, you will be just like them.

You know that condition is contagious." I confessed my ignorance on that point indicating that I was willing to take the risk. Ironically, that man's daughter is now a teacher of the mentally retarded.

Some parents were reluctant to have their children enrolled in special education classes because of the possible stigma that would be attached. Many principals, teachers, and counselors supported the parents in their reluctance. The propaganda was spread that the special education classes were supported by a fabulous funding source, hence there was no need for community support of our fund-raising efforts.

It was believed by many that once a child was admitted to special education classes, he could never be returned to regular classes.

As the program grew it became necessary to house some of our units on other campuses. One principal objected strenuously to this arrangement and told me that as long as he was the principal, there never would be a special education unit on his campus, and there was not. Fortunately for the program, his days were numbered. During that conference, I asked him what he would recommend for servicing children with mental or physical disabilities. His answer was, "Nothing." For one of the few times in my professional life, I lost my professional composure, and angrily retorted, "Well, you can't kill them."

Through indirect pressure that I was able to apply, he did finally consent for one of our students, who had fulfilled graduation requirements, to march in the procession with other graduating students and receive his diploma. When he announced the name of the special education student, he added deliberately, " . . . from the Fourth Ward School of Mental Retardation." His intent to embarrass was evident even to persons who were not aware of the background.

We never developed any formal sophisticated strategies for the solution of our problems, but we unanimously agreed that we needed to interpret our program to the community and we needed to utilize every opportunity to do this. Efforts to interpret the program became a tradition at Fourth Ward School.

One of our first efforts in this direction was to enter an exhibit at the Anderson County Fair. School exhibits were generally entered on a competitive basis, but by special permission our display was entered for "exhibit only." It consisted mainly of specimens of handwriting, art, and handicraft. Since school had been in session little more than a month, our entries were limited both in quality and quantity, but we received favorable public reaction and were quite pleased.

Setting up our booth at the fair became an annual event and the display became more sophisticated. We were always careful to display students' work only. At various times our entries consisted of baked foods, preserves, jellies, wearing apparel, items from the woodworking class, and art objects, as well as specimens of academic work. Our participation in the fair was of tremendous importance to our students. Not only did they have the joy of creating something worthy of pride, they enjoyed the privilege of actually setting up the exhibit. They did the pasting, tacking, and cutting necessary to make our booth one of the most attractive at the fair. And finally they who had known so much failure knew the sweetness of success and the joy of having their success publicly recognized.

Annual fairgoers looked forward each year to seeing how we would give to the public our message of special education. Out of appreciation for the quality of our exhibit and as a means of encouragement, the fair association began to give us a cash donation each year.

In later years some of our students placed individual exhibits in general competition. The entries usually consisted of baked goods, canned goods, and specimens of handicraft, and were of such high quality they generally succeeded in winning prizes. An entry in our school log dated October 3, 1957, reads, "We won five prizes at the county fair."

Both Helen and I understood well that our efforts to interpret the special education program to the community served other purposes also, for our efforts invariably provided image-building experiences for our students and proved to be strong sources of reassurance to parents. To this end, we permitted no recognized opportunity to pass.

Our students were permitted to engage in many activities incident to the daily operation of the school. They painted flower pots, cared for the growing plants, adjusted the window shades, and picked up trash from the campus, which soon earned the reputation of being the best maintained one in the Palestine school district. Students alternated the responsibility of ringing the bell at period changes and were motivated thereby to learn to tell time. Each room conducted its morning devotional under student direction. The pledge to the flag, the Lord's Prayer, Bible verses, rhymes, and simple poetry were learned and recited. Neither Helen nor I possessed any musical ability and our students suffered from our limitations. We presented public programs during American Education Week and Texas Public School Week, but these programs consisted mainly of choral readings, puppet shows, and playlets. These presentations were far from being Broadway productions. They did not even satisfy our standards for special education students, but they brought success experiences to children whose lives had been a succession of failures and frustrations.

Within the realm of reason, we did all we could to provide our children a variety of intensive and extensive experiences. Just before Christmas we asked them if they would like to make a nature-study trip to a farm and select a Christmas tree for the entrance of our building. They adored the idea. So we devoted our science lessons to nature's seasonal changes. We integrated this timely subject with our language-arts materials. We did problems in arithmetic related to our forthcoming trip. The number of students who would make the trip, the number of miles from the school to the farm, the cost of gasoline, and the desired height of our tree all became concerns of our mathematics students.

Pictures were made of us as we left the campus, and more pictures were made of the children as they scampered through the woods in search of the most desirable tree. The *Palestine Herald-Press* for December 6, 1955, carried a small item reporting on our field trip. This incidentally was the first newspaper publicity regarding our work at Fourth Ward. Procurement and decoration of that tree and the exchange of gifts that followed were exciting events for our children and did much to make their Christmas a merry one.

One morning in the spring of 1956, I confronted Helen with the skeleton of a notion that had entered my mind the night before. I asked what she thought of sponsoring an open house as the culminating event for our year's work. She immediately began to make suggestions that added body to my skeleton. Our joint planning soon produced the format for an event far more elaborate than my original idea embodied. Our strategy was to make this our crowning event of the year and in this we were highly successful.

The local press gave advance coverage to the event. Written invitations were sent to parents and other interested citizens. The whole plan was explained to the children with detailed instructions of the roles they were to play. They entered into the spirit of the activities with excitement and anticipation.

May 10, 1956, was truly a red-letter day for our school. Growing plants and cut flowers that had been sent by well-wishers were placed at strategic spots about our rooms and the hall. They added a festive atmosphere to our otherwise drab and colorless old building. There was something on display from every department and each student. A local department store lent us a glass showcase in which to display our layer, loaf, and sheet cakes, and assortment of pies in the entry hall. It was the first thing a visitor saw as he entered the building, and the gasps of unbelief were as eloquent as the many compliments we were to hear during the day. Repeatedly we were asked, "Did these children really do this?"

The positive response by the visitors was not lost on the students. Girls, serving as open-house guides, wore name tags attesting that they had made the dresses they were wearing. With equal pride and a new sense of self-esteem, the boys pointed out flower stands, bookcases, and magazine racks they had made in the woodworking department. Some of the boys wore shirts they had made. Adult hostesses, many of whom were mothers working two-hour shifts, assisted the student guides in conducting visitors through the building. The students' role was extremely important for they could identify each exhibitor, and many visitors desired to see the work of a particular child. There was always noticeable change in a parent's countenance when he viewed the praiseworthy product of his child's effort. To know that his child could do something, whether academic or manual, seemed to enhance the self-worth of the parent. It was as though the child's success clothed the parent with a new respectability.

Punch was served with cookies baked by the students. Both boys and girls dispensed the refreshments with napkins imprinted with "Fourth Ward School Open House 1956."

Press coverage was extremely favorable. The May 10, 1956, issue of the *Palestine Herald-Press* carried an item with the headline, "200 See Fourth Ward Displays." The item reported visitors from three counties representing a variety of occupations.

We had no way of measuring the impact of our open house on public attitude, but we do know that it was positive. Helen and I were pleased. We were so pleased, I am sure our appraisal of the affair was skewed. There must have been some weaknesses in the project that we overlooked in our exuberance. Anyway, we began to have a few telephone calls from parents who wanted to know how to get their children in the special education program. In comparing notes we found that favorable comments and interested questions about special education appeared more frequently in casual conversations.

There was one other event during our first year that probably had some impact on changing attitudes about special education. The City Teachers Association, an all-black organization, held one of its monthly meetings at Fourth Ward School. As the main item on the agenda, Helen and I explained our special education program. Our efforts probably did not significantly increase our following, but at least gave the professional staff members a basic understanding of the philosophy of special education and informed them of the special services available in the Palestine school district.

We chose this occasion too, to give status to our students. The foods classes prepared sandwiches, cookies, punch, and tea, and our older girls served these refreshments to the visitors. Their performance evoked much praise, and of course the girls were exceedingly proud of themselves. I still recall vividly the happiness reflected in the eyes of one of our biplegic girls when she realized that she had indeed performed the duties of a waitress without mishap.

Beyond a doubt, the greatest testimony to the success of our first year's work was the fact that the administration recognized the need for expanded services for mentally retarded and physically disabled children and made plans to meet these needs by adding two more units for black children. The superintendent apprised me of this fact in late spring. Of course, we were delighted. This meant that my group of some sixteen youngsters—ranging in age from seven to seventeen—could be separated into smaller groups with less chronological disparity. It also made possible the recruitment of a music teacher. I was given the responsibility of recruiting and recommending the two additional teachers.

Finding a teacher for the primary-age educable mentally retarded children posed no problem whatever. A former coworker, Mildred Browne—certified in special education and anxious to enter the field—was a natural for this position.

Recruiting the second teacher was a more crucial matter. I knew of no other teacher in the county who was certified in special education. The person chosen, therefore, must be willing to attend summer school. Moreover, my desire to add to our staff a teacher who could develop a strong music department had become an obsession. The combination of these requirements made my recruitment efforts difficult and considerably narrowed the field from which I could choose.

One night the name of Freddie Stanley Wagner flashed through my mind. I knew she possessed the desired attributes, but I had no idea of her willingness to work with mentally retarded children, or of her willingness to attend summer school. Then, too, she was under contract with the Flint Hill district. So, over Frank's very practical admonition that one o'clock in the morning was no time to make a business telephone call, I telephoned Freddie and was gratified to know that she was interested in my proposal.

The superintendent and the board accepted my recommendations and September, 1956, saw the upper story of our building converted into suitable classrooms. No one knew better than I what the addition of Mildred Browne and Freddie Wagner to the Fourth Ward staff would mean to the special education program of the Palestine school district. Once I heard a noted educator say, "You don't build a curriculum, you hire it." I agree with this statement. I knew that I had hired an excellent music curriculum in Freddie and an excellent art curriculum in Mildred.

A piano had been housed in our school building during its period of disuse. We did little during our first year to deliver it from its idle state. I, who could scarcely locate middle C on the keyboard, tried to pick out the treble notes of some simple music. My awkward one-hand performance proved to be so humerous and distracting to the children that it counteracted any musical benefits. I very wisely wrote my efforts off for what they were—complete failure. Thereafter, the service of the piano was limited to its use in demonstrating the correct procedure for dusting and polishing furniture.

When Freddie joined our staff, there was a resurrection of music and the instrument again was pressed into active service. There was a problem, however, as the piano was on the first floor and Freddie's room was on the second. How could we move a piano? Even our custodian was female. But Freddie was adamant in her demands that the piano be moved up to her room. In a casual conversation, I mentioned our plight to a woman who had lived in the neighborhood for almost half a century. She declared, "That's no problem at all. I'll get the piano moved." I trusted her simply because of the sheer force of her personality and the positive quality of her voice. That conversation with Mrs. Josie Helen Derry proved to be epochal. It set off a chain reaction that was to influence special education in Palestine and, to some extent, throughout the state of Texas.

Miss Josie, as she was generally called, was something of an institution in Palestine. Through a collection of yellowed paper clippings she could document interesting bits of little-known or forgotten history. She had made beaten biscuits for the brother of Mrs. Herbert Hoover, and in numerous and sundry ways had befriended the widow of the late John Reagan, former postmaster general of the Confederacy. Her claim was that she had helped to raise some of Palestine's finest men, both black and white. A favorite expression was, "I kissed their cheeks, filled their tummies, and spanked their bottoms." Children were her great love and she found many ways of demonstrating her concern. Naturally children returned her affection.

Miss Josie set a date for the moving of the piano, and she invited a few dependable men to meet her at the school. Among those were Frank, Eugene Dix, E. L. Lane, and Alvo McGriff. On the scheduled date, she arrived at the school about four in the afternoon and took a commanding position at the front door. I soon recognized her strategy. On returning home from work at the end of the day, many of the men of the neighborhood passed by the school. Not one refused her plea when she called out, "Come in here for a few minutes; we need a helping hand." Soon, eight or ten men were assembled; they combined their strength and skill to move the piano up the winding stairs.

The moving of the piano gave the name "Helping Hands" to any person or group of persons that served our program in any way. It ultimately resulted in a formal PTA organization. Because many of our parents had children in other schools and were active in PTA work in those schools, we did not attempt a formal organization during our first years. I think delay in formalizing our relationship did much to insure the success of our PTA once the organization was perfected. As "Helping Hands," parents and citizens had developed a sense of togetherness, and a joint recognition of needs. They also experienced the joy of working in unity to reach a common goal. It was the "Helping Hands" who made the choir robes for all of the students, provided cars to transport students for health examinations and treatment, and collected clothing so there would be a full wardrobe at school to meet emergencies. By the time the PTA was officially organized in September, 1959, the organizational spirit was alive and functioning.

As the Christmas of 1956 approached, our enthusiasm about a public program increased, and so did our determination to make it an event worthy of wide recognition. This year the faculty was not hampered by lack of musical skill. Moreover, we had the capability of a competent art teacher to help with designing costumes and assist the students in the construction of stage property.

Since we had no auditorium and since our presentation was to be religious in nature, we secured the use of a large church auditorium. The forthcoming event was widely publicized, and our classrooms became proverbial beehives of activity. Angels' wings, fashioned sometimes clumsily with spastic hands, were completed and hung at a safe distance from curious kinesthetic impulses. Discarded bedspreads were transformed into shepherds' garb. Cane poles, wire clothes hangers, and teachers' ingenuity and patience combined with youthful eagerness to produce shepherds' staffs. Animals for the manger scene, some of which were life-size, were created through the use of papier-mâché. Lighting effects were developed and were controlled on the night of the presentation by Mildred's husband, Reginald O. Browne, Sr.

Our program was in the form of a pageant and every child in the school had a part in it. A youngster with extremely limited speaking ability could be an effective Wise Man, for his major responsibility was to kneel before the baby Jesus as He lay wrapped in swaddling clothes. Orthopedic children camouflaged their crippling conditions and became as "normal" as others as they stood proudly in their choir robes and sang traditional Christmas carols that accompanied the pantomime and Bible narrative. The pageant was an original arrangement by the staff and was based on the Biblical account of the Nativity.

All our planning and hard work paid dividends. When the curtain rose in the auditorium of the South Union Baptist Church on December 12, 1956, there was standing room only, and in the audience there was representation from all ethnic and interest groups in the city. The children played their parts, according to one admirer, "with a bobble." They were superb.

Looking back now, I am willing to concede that we had perhaps overtrained our youngsters. We literally forced them to a state of near perfection. Our aim, in addition to providing much needed success experiences for all, was to prove to the public that special education students could perform in many fields if accommodations were made for their individual limitations. In this we were highly successful. When the rousing strains of "Joy to the World" ended our performance and the vast audience stood as one to join the final chorus, few eyes were dry—mine perhaps least of all.

As proud as the teachers and the students were, many of the parents were even more proud. Perhaps in the hearts of many was the whispered reassurance, my child is not crazy. He is not a hopeless cripple. He can make a meaningful contribution in a manner that the public recognizes and appreciates.

The Nativity pageant, with some variations, became an annual affair for the Fourth Ward School, and each year the community looked forward to it with joyous anticipation. In later years, under Freddie's direction, the students broadcast Christmas carols over the local radio station and sang at the local homes for the aged. Tape recordings of their renditions were sometimes requested by nursing home residents. These requests were usually fulfilled. Mrs. R. H. McLeod, the widow of a former mayor and the donor of the school's first tape recorder, was especially pleased to receive as a Christmas gift, a recording of the Fourth Ward Choir singing Christmas carols.

Somehow, perhaps through the office of the local superintendent, we learned that it was our responsibility to develop a local plan for special education. We probably could have collected models from other districts throughout the state, but because of extreme naiveté or foolish trust in our own ability we did not. Rather, we decided to pool our own philosophies of special education, our own ideas of the needs of our students, and our own strategies for meeting these needs. Over a period of several weeks, we met routinely on a rotating basis after school hours at our homes. Over coffee and between interruptions by family demands, we developed the first official plan for special education for the Palestine Independent School District. It bore the date 1957-1958.

Perhaps the word, "unorthodox" would aptly describe both the Fourth Ward PTA and its forerunner, the "Helping Hands." We were always more concerned with meeting the specific needs of our community than conforming to the constitutional requirements of the state or national body. We were small in number, as our total membership probably never exceeded thirty, but we were an ambitious group. Two months after our formal organization, we presented Judge Sarah T. Hughes, later in the national spotlight when she administered the presidential oath to Lyndon B. Johnson following the assassination of President Kennedy. She spoke without a fee to a community-wide mass meeting on the "Home Needs of

Children." Many prominent legal figures of our community attended her lecture, and their presence helped to enhance our public image.

Each year our PTA chose a theme that was relevant to some problem area and we developed our annual program around that theme. One year, our theme was "Understanding Your Child." Other themes that I recall were, "My Responsibility," "Toward Better Mental Health," and "Special Education is Everybody's Business." At each monthly meeting, some aspect of the theme would be addressed. Our means of exploring the theme were varied and included symposiums, lectures, panel discussions, films, slide presentations, and skits. We drew on many community resources and at one time or another involved representatives from the legal profession, social service, medicine, the employment commission, religion, the taxing authority, general education, vocational education, department of corrections, and extension service. I do not recall that anyone ever refused an invitation to appear on our program, and no one ever charged for his services. Occasionally we invited persons who worked on the state level and we found these to be equally cooperative.

By working closely with parents, we often were able to identify a family's individual needs, as well as needs that were more or less common to the group. Institutionalizing mentally retarded children was an area of mass concern. Well-meaning friends and relatives had suggested to some parents that their children be placed in an institution. Some parents were haunted by the question of how the child would be cared for after the death of the parent. This was a grave matter, to say the least. Our approach was to study each case on its individual merit, expose the parents to as much professional help as possible, and then let them make their own decision. I can recall only four youngsters from our program who were placed in an institution.

In our efforts to provide a broader understanding of institutional life, we decided to visit the state school at Mexia, Texas. I do not recall the details of how this decision came about. We went by private car and there must have been some twelve or fifteen women in our group. There were no men. The date was April 18, 1959.

This tour proved to be the precursor of eleven others, for it became, like many other successful projects at Fourth Ward School, an annual event. The tours became more sophisticated as time passed and the number of participants increased. After three or four years of using private cars, we began to charter Continental Trailways buses. Men joined our group and there was rarely a vacant seat. Our sphere of interest expanded and we no longer confined our visits to institutions for the mentally retarded. In addition to visiting Marbridge Ranch at Austin and the Denton State School, we visited the School for the Deaf in Austin, the Goodwill Industries in Fort Worth, the Dallas Rehabilitation Institute, John Sealy Hospital, the Moody Cerebral Palsy Center at Galveston, the Shriner's Hospital in Shreveport, Louisiana, and the Beaumont Remedial Center. These tours were gala affairs in all of our lives for our schedule always provided time for sightseeing, shopping, and dining.

Once in Hearne, Texas, during the racially-tense period of Freedom Riders, we stopped for breakfast at a cafe. Each of us wore a small identifying badge made in the shape of a dogwood blossom. We noticed some degree of disorientation on the part of the waitresses, and we attributed it to the size of our group. One of the black workers on duty finally whispered that it was feared that we were a protest group. Evidently, no one ever read our tags, and we made no effort to divest our hostesses of their misconception. We enjoyed a good breakfast in spite of the strained atmosphere and went merrily on our way.

As the spirit of the annual PTA tour intensified, the idea of student tours was born. Our first student tour was made on May 6, 1961, when we went to Fort Worth to visit the zoo and the planetarium. We continued the student tour as an annual activity until a change in administrative policies restricted the use of school buses. Before then, however, we had visited Six Flags Over Texas, the San Jacinto Monument, the Fair Park museums and Love Field in Dallas, the Dixieland Festival in Shreveport, and Galveston, Texas.

I think of our sponsorship of those student tours as one of the most comprehensive projects with which I was involved during my entire teaching career. Although the tours were always made in the spring near the end of the school year, planning for the trip began in early fall. Students in the advanced social studies classes wrote to chambers of commerce in cities they wanted to visit. Sometimes they chose a city that had been suggested by one of the younger children. Upon the receipt of materials from the various chambers of commerce, the students who had written the letters appeared before the entire student body and explained the attractions of their chosen cities. Each child in the school then voted for his choice by secret ballot. Children who could not write voted by whispering the name of their favored city to a teacher.

Once the winning city was announced, the cost of the trip was determined. A letter of request was written by a student and mailed to the transportation department. Mileage was checked. A study was made of the counties and towns through which the group would pass while on tour. Students learned the names of the rivers they would cross and the kinds of trees they could expect to see. The ability to read and interpret highway signs came in for consideration, as well as the time it would take to make the trip.

The children were encouraged to start making installment payments on their fares early. Teachers aided them in keeping records of their deposits and in determining the balance still needed. Clothing students discussed the correct clothing for the tour and the foods students developed suitable menus for picnic lunches for the tour. Possibilities of integrating various learning experiences into the project were almost limitless. Securing parents to assist the teachers with chaperone duties was never a problem.

Every child made the trip regardless of his family's economic status. Cash donations from various organizations and from a few individuals made this possible. Older children needing financial assistance usually found cooperative persons who provided them with employment once their goal was explained. On each tour we counted among our passengers some students who had never been outside of Palestine.

After the use of school buses was restricted, and our units were housed on separate campuses, the advanced students raised funds and chartered buses for their tours. On one occasion, they made an overnight trip to Houston, where many had their first experience in hotel living. It is difficult to say whether the children found more joy in anticipating the trips or in recounting their experiences after the trips were made, but I suspect that every trip is indelibly stamped upon the minds of each participant.

In September, 1965, a half unit for trainable mentally retarded children was organized and Mrs. Zella Watkins, a graduate of Wiley College, was employed to teach them. The advanced group was moved from Fourth Ward to the Story High School campus. Still other major changes were in store for us. On February 6, 1966, Mildred was transferred to the Title I program as a special reading teacher. She was replaced by Mrs. Freta E. Parkes, who resigned a position in a county rural school to accept the post at Fourth Ward.

Our program had now been in operation ten years. We had earned no laurels upon which to rest, but we could list many accomplishments. Many of our earlier problems had been resolved. We had developed more effective strategies for dealing with others. Still others had become more complex, but we had developed confidence in our own ability to cope with them. In our efforts to help our students, their parents, and the general public, we had indeed grown ourselves.

Helen had received a scholarship from the Texas Society for Crippled Children and earned her Master of Education degree from the University of Texas in 1959. Freddie also had earned the master's degree from the same institution in 1961. I had received scholarships from the National Epilepsy League, the National Society for Crippled Children and Adults, and the National Society for the Prevention of Blindness. I had spent two summers studying at Syracuse University and another at my alma mater, San Francisco State Teachers College. Mildred had held the master's degree when she first joined our staff, but she continued her studies in the field of special education at the University of Texas. In our community, we had earned the reputation of being thoroughly prepared and quite knowledgeable in the area of special education.

We regarded the end of our first decade as a sort of milepost and we decided to do a simple follow-up study and see what had happened to our students. The results revealed that in ten years— 1955 to 1965—we had serviced ninety-nine students of which fifty-four were male and forty-five were female. Fourteen students had returned to regular classes, seven of which returned without the recommendation of a professional referral committee. Nine had graduated from regular high school and thirteen had received high school diplomas as graduates of special education classes. There were fifteen known dropouts. Five former students had entered military service. Two orthopedic students had entered college and twenty-three had received or were receiving vocational training. Four were institutionalized in state schools and one was in a correctional institution. Three were deceased. Thirteen were married, two were separated, and one was divorced.

10

REJECTED STONES

O NE OF THE bothersome realities of educa-
tional measurement is the inability of the process to identify all
factors that may influence the behavior of the subject, and the degree to which any factor may be operative. Conversely, we have
yet to perfect an instrument that can determine with absolute cer-
tainty what the behavior of a subject would have been had there
been no intervention. Faced with this situation, planners in special
education, like those in traditional education, can never be sure
whether or not special education programs should receive credit
for the success of special education students. By the same token,
one wonders if it is fair to blame special education for the many
failures of special education students. So, as I analyze the feedback
from former students, I try to do so with a degree of sober detach-
ment, allowing myself neither the joy of personal satisfaction nor
the sting of private guilt.

In spite of these recognized constraints, one popular means of
evaluating the quality of an institution's offerings is to study its
products. A special education program then may conceivably be
evaluated by the same means. From the inception of our program,
the analysis of feedback from our ex-students and graduates has
proved to me most interesting.

However I have viewed the situation, I have found that remarkable success stories have come from unlikely quarters and that some
miserable failures have resulted in areas that had seemed promising.

As would be expected in a normal group, the reports of extreme success and of profound failure are about equal in number with the majority of the reports falling between the two extremes.

Looking in retrospect at the many young people I encountered during my many years of teaching, I can think of three boys only whom I would without any qualms classify as "bad boys." Two of these I met as special education students. During one period I had both enrolled in my educable mentally retarded class at the same time. I needed no super understanding of children nor any special training in psychology to predict that these boys would not grow up to be successful citizens. One has already served a short prison term, and at this writing the other is in an East Coast jail awaiting trial.

To those of us who were familiar with the lifestyle of the P. family, it was no surprise to learn that two of the daughters became pregnant about the same time, possibly by the same man. When the parents made inquiry as to the identity of the responsible male, both girls' answer was the same—"That brown-skinned boy."

Twelve-year-old T. withdrew from my educable mentally retarded class because of pregnancy, so there was no surprise a few weeks later when she rang the bell at my home and passed to me her neatly wrapped baby and said, "Here, Mrs. Robinson, I brought you a baby boy." The child's guilelessness, and her utter lack of shame combined with a total ignorance of the responsibility of motherhood disconcerted me. All I could say was, "No, T., you did not have the baby for me. It is yours." T.'s mother took care of the baby and she was permitted to return to school. The surprise came with her subsequent pregnancies. Now twenty-five years of age, she has five sons and has never been married.

I was not shocked when M. was found guilty of breaking and entering, for as a student in my class evidence often linked him with missing items. It was no surprise either when S. was sent to the state correctional institution for girls, because even as a student she spent so many nights away from home. Her grandmother, who was also her guardian, gave up in despair.

In spite of my experience and my efforts to maintain a detached professional approach to my work, there were some episodes that shocked me deeply. One such incident occurred when a young mentally retarded couple reported the sale of their baby to secure funds for bus fare home from West Texas where they had been picking cotton. I experienced a second shock when I learned that two of our mentally retarded students who were parents of two children and were maintaining a household, were not married, but were merely "shacking up." This overt defiance of moral and legal concepts both shocked and disappointed me.

By far the most frustrating and futile effort I spent in connection with my work in special education centers around a young woman who was enrolled in my first class. Twenty years later, I am still indirectly concerned with her and her problems. On September 20, 1955, I wrote a short narrative about W. indicating that she was operating below grade one in all basic skills; she dressed very untidily and possessed an extremely obnoxious body odor.

Anecdotal records covering a period of five years indicate peaks and valleys in W.'s academic growth, but there was almost no improvement in her personal grooming habits. Once the bus driver threatened to withdraw her bus riding privileges so offensive was her body odor. Using a number three laundry tub, we set up a regular bathing routine for W. at school. We even kept a wardrobe of several complete changes of clothing for her benefit, but all of these efforts resulted in no permanent change. She left public school at age nineteen, but continued to receive training in domestic work in the vocational rehabilitation program. One happy day, a note came announcing the engagement of W. Frankly I wondered who would marry her. About two years and two or three children later an invitation came to attend the wedding ceremony. I was thoroughly confused and indicated as much to W.'s mother. She explained that the license had run out, but the children were really going to get married this time.

To this day, I am in no position to verify the legal status of that couple, but they are the parents of eleven children of whom nine are living. At one point, the welfare department saw fit to place some of the children in a foster home because the parents had failed to care for them properly. That the children lack care is a documented fact. Various welfare organizations as well as private citizens have repeatedly come to the family's aid with food supplies, clothing, and household furnishings. Articles of clothing frequently are lost; the children play with canned goods as though they were toys, and the house in which the family lives has burned more than once. There seems to be no means of helping this family solve its problems. I wonder if the next generation will bring a solution or more problems.

When I learned that one of our students had landed a position on the police force in a nearby small city, I was delighted. Knowing his home environment, I was surprised that he would aspire to such a post, and knowing his scholastic limitations I was equally surprised that he could pass the test.

Z. was a young girl who came to Fourth Ward School on her knees. For some deep psychological reason, she was of the opinion that she could not walk. She kept her head tied up Aunt Jemima-fashion and her total attempt at verbal communication was limited to a high-pitched yes or no. The local Kiwanis Club sent Z. and her father to a psychiatric clinic at John Sealy Hospital in Galveston, Texas. The psychiatric staff reported absolute noncooperation on the part of the subject. A second session in the absence of the father was suggested. This was arranged with Helen accompanying the girl and the Kiwanis Club again financing the effort. On this visit, Z. was more cooperative and remained as a patient at the clinic for several weeks. One day the telephone at the school rang and in her still high-pitched voice, Z. announced that she was ready to return. This was really a high moment for us all. Upon her return to school she was placed on the vocational rehabilitation training program for domestic workers. Later, Z. moved to California. One day several years later, a neatly dressed, self-assured, articulate young woman arrived at Helen's front door. It was our long-lost Z. She reported that she was now happily married and had brought her young daughter to visit the teacher who had played such an important role in her life.

Perhaps our most incredible success story concerns a young man who is employed by the sanitation department of one of Texas's largest cities. He came to us as a youngster of seven years, bringing along a report card that bore the words, "This child has never said a word in school." He was definitely the most withdrawn human being I have ever known. A whole semester passed before he would even whisper. I think he was startled the first time he heard his own voice. I know the first time I heard it, I cried. H. could not be induced to sit at his desk. Rather he sat under it. When other children joined in group play on the campus, he hid behind trees. Slowly—very slowly—this young boy yielded to careful nurturing. He remained in the special education program until a few weeks prior to his scheduled graduation when he passed the entrance test for military service, and was immediately inducted.

After discharge he got married and secured his present job, and is apparently leading a happy, normal life. To this day I do not know whether H.'s major problem was mental retardation, but I feel very strongly that it was a fortunate thing for him that he and special education were brought together.

When one of our students secured work at a slaughtering plant and paid more income taxes one year than his former teacher did, we considered it an occasion for great rejoicing.

One of our students has completed several years of satisfactory service as a teacher's aide in the Houston public schools. One young man is a mechanic in the service department of a large distributor of General Motors automobiles. Another is the chief mechanic for a local school district with responsibility for keeping the fleet of school buses in running order. The baker at a local hospital is one of our former students, as is the fry-cook at a drive-in cafe. The head maintenance person at a large church received vocational training through our program. Two of our students hold barber's licenses and two are in the ministry. The chef at a leading local hotel told me recently that the best kitchen helpers he had were those who had been trained through our vocational rehabilitation program.

We graduated three students with significant hearing losses. One was killed in an accident shortly after graduation. One works as a cook in a restaurant, and the third young man moved to California where, according to his family, he maintains a beautifully appointed apartment, works in food service for a major West Coast cafeteria chain, and drives his own Cadillac.

These brief references give some evidence that we have tasted both the bitter and the sweet of educational endeavor. Twenty years ago, a subject hotly debated by educators and budget people alike centered around the amount of money spent on special education programs as compared to that spent on programs for the so-called normal children. Opposition to the amount of money spent on special education students held that it represented a poor investment because these students would never be able to pay their way and they would always be tax liabilities.

Our findings reveal a situation not too different from that involving the normal school population. We have examples of both successes and failures and, between these two extremes, our ranks of mediocrity are filled.

11

THE EYES OF TEXAS

I SUPPOSE FEW EVENTS that significantly affect the lives of people occur abruptly and without forewarning; it only seems so because the individual's involvement in a swirl of activity makes prediction and assessment difficult. I think this describes our position during our early years at Fourth Ward School. I do not know at what point our program began to draw statewide attention, but our awareness of it came rather abruptly and rather surprisingly.

I feel certain that not one of us ever planned or pursued an undertaking with the aim of impressing the Texas Education Agency or any other state agency. We went about our work moving from one activity to another with the sole purpose of meeting a need as we perceived it.

We were wholly ignorant then as to the reason a representative of the state agency, while passing through our city, stopped at Fourth Ward and congratulated each of us individually. In explanation, she told us that a copy of our local plan for special education had been placed on display by the Special Education Department of the Texas Education Agency and that it was considered one of the best local plans in the state.

One evening a few weeks later, as we sat at dinner, Frank recounted an interesting dialogue that had taken place that day between him and a special education consultant from the Texas Education Agency. At that time, Frank was serving as superintendent of the Butler Independent School District. His special education department was having some difficulty that no doubt was common to many new programs. Anyway, a consultant had been invited to visit the department. After giving some on-site assistance, she sought to give further aid by suggesting a model special education department that the Butler teachers could visit. She chose Palestine. Since the Butler school was only twenty-two miles from Palestine, her suggestion may have been influenced as much by geography as by the quality of our program. She said to Frank, "The Palestine program is headed by a Mrs. Dorothy Robinson. Do you know her?" Frank said that he could not resist his reply which was, "I sleep with her every night." When the laughter subsided, she said, "Well, there you have all the help you need."

The practice of recommending the Fourth Ward program as a model became widespread. We began to receive calls stating that an agency representative had suggested a visit to our school. We have records of visits from teachers at Whitehouse, Oakwood, Jacksonville, Teague, Diboll, Fairfield, Coolidge, and Corsicana. Following the visit of the Corsicana group, we received this letter:

Corsicana Public Schools
Corsicana, Texas
January 17, 1958

Mrs. Dorothy Robinson
4th Ward Special Education School
Palestine, Texas

Dear Mrs. Robinson:

Our teachers appreciated the very cordial reception they received from you and your staff on their recent visit. They seemed to get a good bit from spending the day with you, and we appreciate your taking time to help them.

Sincerely yours,

Robert Ashworth
Superintendent of Schools

Today the special education program of the Corsicana school district is very highly regarded throughout the state. My sister-in-law, Mrs. Warner James Redus, whom I encouraged to enter the field of special education, is the supervisor of the Corsicana program. She is possibly the only black special education supervisor in the state of Texas.

In the fall of 1958, Prairie View College, my alma mater, asked me to join its extension staff in Palestine and teach a course in special education. My class of some thirty students represented six counties.

I had no secretary or receptionist at Fourth Ward, so our youngsters frequently answered the telephone and as often as possible received and relayed messages. Many of the students became quite adroit at this. So one day when a call came from the Texas Education Agency in Austin, the child who answered knew that this was beyond his parameter. I was called to the telephone.

Don Partridge of the Special Education Department was calling to invite me to work with a team to develop new guidelines for special education. I accepted without knowing the details. He explained that the team would work at East Texas State University at Commerce, Texas, for a period of not more than six weeks and that college credits would be given to the participants. There was also some provision for reimbursement. I was delighted with the offer. Here was a chance for me to enhance my professional growth and at the same time inculcate some of my philosophy and ideas of special education into state guidelines. Participation in this project would also enable me to satisfy a requirement of my local school district that at specified intervals all teachers must show evidence of professional growth. Additional study was accepted as that evidence.

My coworkers were delighted too, for they considered this "our" good fortune. In making the announcement, the local news media considered it an honor for the Palestine school district.

So the summer of 1966 saw me off to East Texas State University. With the cooperation of the Texas Education Agency, our team completed its six weeks' work in about half that time. Some months later *Guidelines For Program Development Bulletin 673* was released. It is highly possible that that publication never received widespread usage, for it was soon supplanted by guidelines for Plan A.

One morning in early 1968, I stopped for my mail on the way to school. There was the usual junk mail and a few pieces that I recognized as being important. But there was one rather voluminous letter whose return address was unfamiliar to me. The sender appeared to be someone connected with MSA; but MSA—whoever it was, or whatever it was—was equally unfamiliar to me. I read the letter and was overwhelmed by two aspects of its contents.

I was being invited to serve as a member of a technical advisory committee to work on a service project that was being conducted by Management Services Associates. The purpose of the project was to provide a basis for recommending changes in the special education program for the state of Texas.

To me this was an awesome responsibility. Who was I to serve on such an august body? What ideas did I have that could possibly be of merit in this gigantic undertaking? What experiences and thoughts did I have that were worth sharing?

I was further awed by the honorarium that was quoted—$100 per day! I had, of course, received honoraria before for various professional services, but the figure had never before reached that level. Fools rush in, I reminded myself. But then I was not rushing in. I was being invited, and I responded with this letter:

P.O. Box 1212
Palestine, Texas
March 8, 1968

Mr. Aris A. Mallas
Management Services Associates
2209 Hancock Drive
Austin, Texas

Dear Sir:

I thank you for your letter of March 8, 1968 in which you described what appears to be a most exciting undertaking. I am both pleased and honored that I have been considered as a member of the Technical Advisory Committee.

I accept the invitation to serve on this committee, and I sincerely hope that I shall be able to make a worthy contribution to such a significant project.

My telephone during business hours is 214/729-2884. My number at home is 214/723-3219.

I assure you that I shall stand ready to respond to any call whenever I am needed.

> *Very truly yours,*
> *(Mrs.) Dorothy R. Robinson*

The first meeting was set for three o'clock on March 29, 1968. I went to Austin by train. That trip incidentally was one of my last trips by rail, as passenger service through Palestine was soon discontinued. At 2:57 P.M. I knelt on the floor of my room in the Sheraton Crest Hotel and asked God to help me make meaningful and helpful contributions to that committee. At three, I entered the courtesy suite where several members of the group had already assembled. At that time I was the only female present; I was also the only black. Every person in the room was a complete stranger to me. But some of the most cherished and the most meaningful friendships of my life were born in that hotel room on that afternoon.

My work on the MSA project was followed by an invitation to serve on the Advisory Council for ESEA (Elementary and Secondary Education Act), Title III Projects. I accepted the invitation with the understanding that I would represent the handicapped. I am at this writing still a member of that council, although the scope of its responsibilities has undergone some changes through the years.

Invitations to accept membership on various committees and requests to provide consultant services became so numerous I was forced to decline some. It was as though a few seeds had been sown and a bountiful harvest had resulted.

The great number of calls that I received should not be taken solely as a testimony to my ability. Many projects were financed by federal funds, and the inclusion of minority representation was often mandated. I happened to be one of the few black professionals with whom state level people were acquainted. Consequently many of my calls resulted from situational emergencies and not from my personal popularity, or my professional expertise. I read in this circumstance a dual opportunity. By recommending members of my staff to fill roles that I declined, I could provide them with an opportunity for greater exposure, and at the same time I could acquaint state-level people with more black professionals for whom they may well have had need.

Soon Mildred was serving on the Continuing Advisory Committee for Special Education, and Freddie was holding membership on a statewide committee concerned with improving the employment status of the physically handicapped. Helen, who had substituted for me on several occasions, was elected minority representative for Texas Classroom Teachers Association and, still later, she was elected to membership in the Black Caucus of NEA.

I was gratified with the numerous opportunities we had to serve in the broader professional arena, and I was especially delighted with the contributions my coworkers were making. At all times, we exercised discretion in accepting outside assignments, for after all, we were under contract to the Palestine Independent School District. We did not engage in any pursuits that demanded an unreasonable amount of time or in any way reduced the effectiveness of our work on the local level. On the contrary, we tried to use the information and ideas garnered from our broader contacts to enrich our own program. Our local officials were aware of our efforts in this regard and approved of our additional professional involvement.

So in fairness and loyalty to our home district, and as a matter of plain common sense, we still found it necessary to decline some invitations. One that I could not regret, and one that I still regard as being epochal, came to me a few days after Governor Preston Smith took the oath of office. A representative of the Texas Education Agency called and said that Governor Smith wondered if I would consider serving on the Advisory Council for Technical–Vocational Education. Would I? Was I dreaming? I followed my usual mode of operation and said yes before I clearly understood the responsibilities associated with my acceptance.

The council held its first meeting on March 4, 1969, with Gover-Smith giving the charge. The membership of the council at that time numbered twenty-one and was composed of representatives from various disciplines, and associating with people of that caliber was always a stimulating experience. When my first term expired, Governor Dolph Briscoe honored me with reappointment. In 1974, the members of the council elected me to the vice-chairmanship, and the following year, I was named to head the council, a position that I hold at this writing.

The membership of the council has now been increased to twenty-four, and with their support and that of the office staff based in Austin, the council has become a viable force for technical–vocational education in Texas, and is exerting some influence on the national scene.

12

THE TWAIN MEET

STEPS TOWARD DESEGREGATION were taken in the Palestine school district as early as 1967. The efforts were fraught with quiet uneasiness and apprehension. People fashioned their individual fears. The old unfounded myths involving racism became grotesque specters that haunted the minds of both black and white. The Mexican–American population in Palestine at that time was relatively small and was generally regarded as being a non-entity or was not regarded at all.

A few white teachers had been assigned to predominantly black schools and a few black teachers had been assigned to predominantly white schools. Apparently in each case the minority teachers were accepted with professional reserve, and they operated more or less as marginal members of their respective faculties. They performed their necessary teaching functions but engaged in little else that tended to strengthen lines of communications.

At one time "freedom of choice" was practiced. This practice made it possible for parents to choose to send their children to any school on their level irrespective to its racial identity. I do not know of one white parent who chose to send his child to a black school, and there were very few black parents who elected to send their children to white schools.

There were some black parents who honestly felt that white teachers, by virtue of being white, were more competent than black teachers. There were others who seemed to feel that their prestige was enhanced by sending their children to a white school. One black mother was heard to say to her neighbor, "Girl, we are living high. We've got Patties teaching our kids." In discussing her attitude, another black mother of more sober intent told me, "I prayed before I sent my girl to the white school. I watches—and they plays with her."

Both freedom of choice and teacher exchange as practiced by the Palestine school district failed to satisfy the demands of the Department of Health, Education, and Welfare (HEW). It became increasingly apparent to all concerned that more concrete steps had to be taken. As this knowledge became prevalent, apprehension grew. Many whites felt that white ladyhood would be in constant jeopardy if white girls were placed in close contact with young black males. There were some whites who felt that black teachers, by virtue of cultural traits and limited professional training facilities, just had to be inferior. Some black parents feared that their children would be abused or otherwise unjustly treated by prejudiced white teachers. Other blacks did not fear mental or physical abuse, but they did feel that white teachers would not work conscientiously and patiently with black children, because they either were not interested in their progress or they felt that they were incapable of learning and therefore efforts to teach them represented a waste of time.

Teachers, too, were haunted by the specter of change. Some white teachers felt that a black teacher on the staff could offer very little professionally, and therefore would simply be dead weight. Still others felt that black teachers would come poorly prepared, and altruistically planned to help them overcome their deficiencies by giving special assistance.

Perhaps the average black teacher entertained some feelings of inferiority. Many doubted their ability to cope with the adjustments necessary to effect desegregation. Personally, the promise of change held no terror for me. Of course, I was concerned. Although it had not happened in our district, I knew numerous cases in which black teachers were dismissed for no reason other than they were black. Teachers with several years' tenure who had earned reputations as strong professionals, and whose contracts were renewed year after year, suddenly became inefficient or too old when the schools were desegregated. Many black teachers took early retirement rather than work in an integrated situation, or face the possibility of an embarrassing dismissal.

I entertained some rather strong feelings about my destiny in the integration process, and I frequently stated my position by saying, "I won't say that I won't be fired, but I am going to make my dismissal difficult to explain. I'm going to be very sure that I am fired because I am black and for no other reason." I had always set very high standards for myself as a teacher and had always worked hard to achieve those standards, but to support my attitude I felt it expedient to evaluate my efforts more critically. I even took the National Teacher Examination that was very much in vogue about that time, and reputedly was used on occasions as a measure of teacher competence. I placed the record of my creditable score in my safe-deposit box, where it still rests. My professional file never contained any record of my having taken the examination. It was an ace in the hole in case it was ever needed.

It is relatively easy to procure data describing the feelings and attitudes of teachers and parents about desegregation. To access the gut feelings of students is quite another matter. It was the students who were the most vulnerable. It was they who stood to gain or lose the most from the change. To get an in-depth story of their experiences and feelings during this traumatic period, society will have to wait until the literature, art, and music of that generation gains public notice.

Desegregation could be legislated, but integration does not lend itself to legislative acts. Anyone who gave a modicum of attention to occurrences during the early years of desegregation in Texas must be aware of this. The change must have been very traumatic for students of both races, and it certainly was for black students. They were the ones who usually gave the most—who lost their identity. In essence they must have questioned themselves as did the exiles in David's Psalms when they asked, "How shall we sing the Lord's song in a strange land?" In most instances, students in the upper grades were transferred to the white school where they felt alien. They forfeited their school songs, yells, colors, offices, and positions of leadership in student organizations. If they remained on their original campus, a new white principal frequently was assigned. If the black principal remained, there often was such an influx of white teachers, the whole complexion of the school's activities was subject to drastic changes. Even the name of the school was subject to change if it honored a black person.

Very little real effort has been made to achieve true integration in Texas schools. Some practices tend to further segregate the two groups. The scarcity of black girls on drill teams, the reduced number of blacks in high school bands, choral groups, honor societies, and honor rolls cannot serve minority students in any meaningful way. Often when white principals were assigned to buildings that previously housed black students, little regard and respect were shown for the school's traditions and achievements. Trophies earned in athletic and literary contests have been discarded as rubbish. This flagrant desecration of revered symbols extended to other departments of the school. One white librarian assigned to a middle school that had originally served black students found the library well stocked with books, tapes, and filmstrips about black people. She wondered who was "foolish enough to waste money on such junk." With that, she proceeded to remove the items from the shelves.

It was in this general setting near the end of the term in 1969 that all elementary teachers in the Palestine district received a special order from the superintendent's office. The order directed each elementary teacher to pack all of her personal belongings and instructional materials. We read this to mean that wholesale moving was in the offing. Teachers said one to the other, "This is it," meaning this is in fact desegregation.

Throughout the summer, teachers engaged in much speculation. Leaks were numerous, and those who trusted the credibility of the leaks probably created for themselves some unnecessary tension and worry.

One day the superintendent asked me if I would be interested in the principalship of one of the primary schools. I replied in the affirmative.

As the opening date of school drew near, and no official announcement of teacher assignments had been made, the tension increased and speculation ran rampant. Although the uncertainty was frustrating, many people felt that the superintendent was exercising strategic diplomacy for, by delaying public announcement until the last minute, he was minimizing the possibility of protests from both the geneneral public and school personnel. Everyone knew that the information had to be released before school started, so concerned people simply waited and engaged in a sort of emotional countdown.

The first information I received about my own assignment was unofficial but surprisingly accurate and it reached me through a medium that bordered on the weird. My telephone rang one afternoon and a neighbor's voice urgently pleaded, "Come over here right away; I have something to show you. I don't care what you are doing. Drop it and come on." Of course, I responded to such a persuasive approach.

When I arrived, she showed me a paper on which the assignment of all black principals and many black teachers had been hurriedly written. The writing was clearly not hers, and when I inquired as to the source of the information, she said, "I cannot tell you now, so please don't ask." I asked no further questions, but there were questions still in my mind. I wondered about the source but, even more, I wondered about the reliability of the listings, according to which I had been assigned the principalship of Rusk Elementary School. Time was to prove that the list was uncannily accurate. A few days after I saw the list, the official assignment was released by the superintendent. I had indeed been named principal of Rusk Elementary School. I knew then that the credibility of the clandestine list was firmly established, but years passed before I learned the source.

The list had come to my friend by the historical servant-quarters route. A domestic worker had seen a record of the school board action with respect to teaching assignments. She hastily copied what she could and passed it to a friend. Her friend passed it to my friend, and my friend shared its contents with me.

Under the total desegregation plan of our district, Rusk Elementary School that had been built in 1938 and had served white students since that time, was to become one of four schools in the district to serve primary grades only. These four schools were then called primary schools instead of elementary schools.

The Rusk school was located in a white residential neighborhood that had yielded its prestigious image to newer and more expensive housing developments. The area was also in ethnic transition. Most of the Mexican-American residents in Palestine lived in that area, and blacks were gradually moving in on the periphery. There were some pessimistic beliefs that more racism existed in that section of our city than in any other, and there was no scarcity of people to tell me so. Usually remarks of that nature were followed by an encouraging statement expressing confidence in my ability to cope with any possible racist developments.

I spent my last four years of teaching in that school and I never encountered a case of overt racism. I am sure some of the residents entertained, among their many human biases, some racial prejudices, but their patriotism, Christianity, or plain common sense seemed to have influenced their relationship with me. The same could be said of the teachers with whom I worked. There were some personnel changes from year to year, but I always enjoyed a pleasant working relationship with my staff members. I feel that areas of conflict that I observed or experienced had their roots in individual differences or in differences of opinion and in no way represented resentment directed to me as a black person.

I was not the only person on the Rusk school staff who had received prior knowledge of my assignment. One white also had received the information. I never knew her source. Anyway, early the day the official announcement was made public, she called me, offered her congratulations, and pledged her support and cooperation.

When I received the official list of my staff members, I called each one, solicited her cooperation, and relayed my hopes for a successful and pleasant working relationship. That first year my staff consisted of seven white and two black teachers. At the paraprofessional level, there were one and one-half whites.

At our first staff meeting, my first act was to pray for divine guidance and blessings. Then I made a few remarks about my basic principles of operation. I described myself as a democratic principal

Above, the Green Bay High School faculty, janitor, and dietitian, 1949-50. Below, my sixth- and seventh-grade students at Green Bay High School, 1949-50.

In the early 1950s I chaired a countywide reading project. A consultant, Mrs. A.C. Preston of Prairie View College, is at the head of the table. I am to her immediate left.

The faculty of the Fourth Ward (special education) school from 1956 to 1965. Back row, left to right, Mildred A. Browne and Helen S. Hooper; front row, left to right, Freddie Wagner and myself.

Above, the special class for orthopedically-handicapped students, and opposite, a special class for the educable mentally retarded, Fourth Ward School, Palestine, Texas, 1955-56.

Fourth Ward School PTA, Palestine, Texas, 1959. I am fifth from the left, front row.

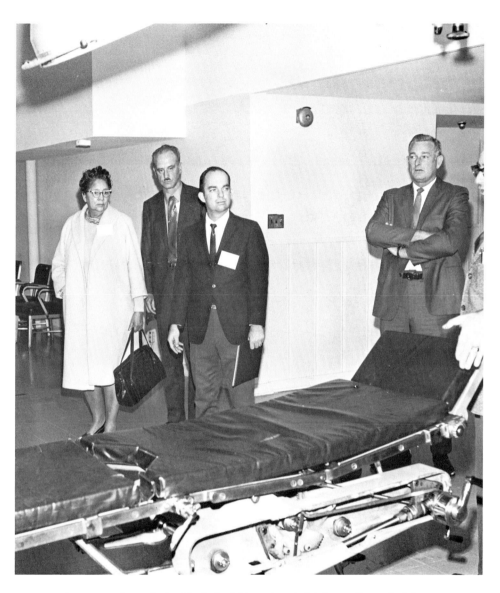

As a member of the Technical–Vocational Advisory Council, I have toured various training facilities including the Texas State Technical Institute at Waco, Texas, late 1960s.

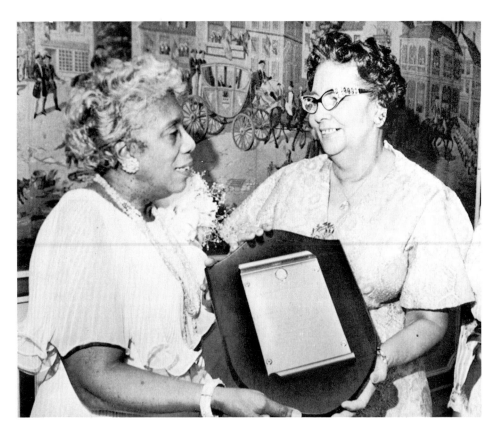

Rosalie McGuire, president of the National Association of Negro Business and Professional Women's Clubs, Inc., presents me with the National Achievement Award in Washington, D.C., August 16, 1975.

Right, I acknowledge a gift after speaking before the Houston League of Business and Professional Women, April, 1970. Below, I am presented a plaque from the Texas Vocational–Technical Association, July, 1975, for my contributions to vocational education.

I delivered the commencement address at Brazosport College, Lake Jackson, Texas, May 15, 1976. Dr. J.R. Jackson, president of the college, is to my left.

Fort Worth Star Telegram

Texas state representative, Paul Ragsdale, right, presents Frank and me
with a plaque for political leadership from Prairie View oriented agriculture teachers, Fort Worth, Texas, August 4, 1976.

Frank J. Robinson, June 7, 1902–October 13, 1976.

Testifying before the Committee on Higher Education, Austin, Texas, September 1, 1976.

Left, three of my students help me pack my belongings in preparation for the long-awaited day of my retirement, Palestine, Texas, May 3, 1974. Below, with my last class of students on my sixty-fifth birthday, May 3, 1974. Opposite, the annual report from the Advisory Council for Technical–Vocational Education is presented to Governor Dolph Briscoe of Texas, June 15, 1976. Left to right: David Pickett, Bill Elkins, myself, Governor Briscoe, Joe Gunn, Elton Thomas, Angie Grace, and Don Rogers.

In June, 1978, I participated in the National Security Seminar at the U.S. War College, Carlisle Barracks, Carlisle, Pennsylvania. My nephew, Colonel Carlly Alton, is on the extreme right of the second row.

with a strong classroom orientation. I invited input, pledged my cooperation and support, and the best leadership of which I was capable. I promised fair and impartial consideration of all issues, but I emphasized that the final and authoritative decisions would always be mine to make and that once such decisions were made, I expected them to be honored.

I candidly discussed our biracial situation. I made two analogies that illustrated the fact that I expected each teacher to teach all children with equal diligence, and if possible to love all children without regard for race, financial standing, or social status. I also suggested that those of us who found it shocking to work with one of a different color should look closely at each other. Stare if necessary, but try to get rid of the shock before the children enrolled. I did not want the children to see *white teachers* or *black teachers*. I wanted them to see *good teachers*.

My new title was teaching principal, for in our district principals of the primary schools also had teaching duties.

It had been some thirty years since I had worked with young children and I admit having had some trepidation about relating to them, but my fears were unfounded. From the beginning my office was filled daily with a conglomerate of Americana—beautiful black, white, and brown children. Each, with the disarming innocence of childhood, came to show me a new sweater, give me a horned lizard, tell me of the birth of a new baby, recount some family tragedy, or simply give me a good-morning embrace. Once a teacher wondered why I let the children " . . . hang around the office for they might break something." I responded by telling her that I felt a few minutes of fellowship with the children was most profitable, for it was then that we learned to know and love each other as people and not necessarily as teacher and students or principal and students. So my relationship with my new multiracial group of students was what my relationship with students had always been generally, and that was pleasant and mutually satisfying.

Students are the most efficient ambassadors a school can have, and my Rusk school children were excellent liaison persons. Many white and Mexican parents met me for the first time with a smile and a happy remark about how their children felt about me. The proof of my acceptance by the parents was further demonstrated when they began to request that their children be assigned to my homeroom. It was also gratifying to note that other black teachers on the staff were receiving similar requests. Then when black parents began to specify their preference for a certain white teacher, I felt that our parents were looking for results and not skin color. For me as principal, this was a happy state of affairs.

Historically, the Rusk school had had an active PTA. During the years I served as principal the official staff of our PTA was racially mixed. Our program was not elaborate, but it was timely and effective; moreover, we demonstrated that a common concern for the welfare of all children can take precedence over racial differences. I would describe the total atmosphere of the Rusk school during my time there as pleasant and positive. This is not to say, however, that we had no problems.

I suppose that all teachers in newly segregated schools experience in varying degrees many of the same problems. There was the shock that usually accompanies new experiences. The very physical closeness of blacks and whites was a new experience for many. For a white teacher to be physically close to her black maid was common, but to be close to a black woman, regard her as an equal, and share a common professional role, represented a different kind of relationship. Children experienced similar shock. As they began to feel more comfortable with each other, it was interesting to see them tactually examine the hair texture of members of the opposite race. Physical incompatibility sometimes existed between children and teachers. Students who felt physically comfortable with a teacher of their own ethnic identity were often shy and withdrawn when the situation demanded a similar relationship with teachers of another race. By the same token, some teachers who were professionally well trained and dedicated to the cause of teaching sometimes found it difficult to submit to physical contact with children of a different race.

Trepidation was the constant companion of many teachers during those early years. Black teachers were tense and uncertain. Many who had years of successful teaching to their credit wondered if they could teach white children satisfactorily. White teachers who knew equally well that they were competent wondered if they could find the strategies necessary to teach black children effectively. After all, the misconception that blacks were intellectually inferior and were therefore difficult to teach was well entrenched.

The prospect of parent conferences posed additional problems for many teachers. Black teachers were prone to believe that white parents would treat them with condescension or contempt; and white teachers feared that black parents would approach the conference situation with hostility. The sad fact is there was a great deal of truth in the suspicions of each group.

Most problems of whatever nature tended to dissipate with increased association and communication. From the point of view of the black community, my personal success in a desegregated situation was a foregone conclusion. As time passed, white citizens seemed to concur. Reactions from a white student, a white teacher, and a white parent exemplify this feeling.

I have among my most cherished mementoes of my teaching career a note from a white, second-grade girl that was written during the 1972-73 school year:

Well, I think Mrs. Dorothy R. Robinson is about the best woman there is. She is also a good teacher, if I do say so myself. She works very hard. She has two jobs and she is very good at both. I love her very much. The End.

During my first semester at the Rusk school, a white teacher on the staff, who had worked under several principals, said to me, "I just want you to know that Dorothy Robinson is the best thing in the way of a principal that has ever happened to me." I thanked her and said, "I hope you can say that at the end of the school year. I assure you I am not assuming a role. I am being myself." Four years later when I retired from the profession, the same teacher said, "Mrs. Robinson, I have no reason to change my early opinion of you." This to me was one of the finest compliments that I received during my entire teaching career.

One day near the end of my last year, a white father came to school to pick up his son. He mentioned my forthcoming retirement and expressed regret that his son would no longer have what he termed " . . . the benefit of associating with you." Then he said, "To me, you are an example of Proverbs 31:10." Having read the book of Proverbs many times, I knew that I had read that scripture, but I could not recall the wording. As soon as he departed, I picked up my Bible and read: "Who can find a virtuous woman? For her price is far above rubies."

13

CURTAINS

O<small>N THE FIRST DAY</small> of the 1973-74 school year, I attached a small bulletin board to the wall above my desk and pinned upon it the numerals *190*. This indicated that my teaching career would end at the expiration of 190 days. I changed the numbers each day to indicate my remaining time. Staff members stopped by frequently to check my status and to predict that I would abandon the project before the school year ended. When only a zero appeared on May 31, 1974, they expressed amazement that I had indeed followed through to the completion of my countdown.

For years I had told friends that May 3, 1974, would mark my sixty-fifth birthday, and on that date I planned to have several large boxes in my office and classroom in which to begin moving my personal belongings home. My friend Geraldyne E. Hunter, who, in addition to being a very competent homemaking teacher, is a very competent photographer, appeared at my office on April 29 and reminded me of my vow and asked to make a picture of me in the process of packing my belongings. I was surprised that she remembered my statement in that regard, but I was pleased that she came to capture the event on film. Little did I know how that picture would be used.

Contrary to the plight of many people who approach retirement, I was both physically and emotionally prepared for the changes retirement would demand. I had long since reconciled myself to the knowledge that I would never be financially ready.

I had literally worked all my life. My childhood was a working childhood. I do not remember a time when I did not have some simple responsibility. As a preschool child, I had served as baby sitter for younger siblings. At the age of eight, I carried a major share of the work involved in the preparation of the family meals. When I reached seven, we were living in a community where there was no school for black children, and because bus transportation was unheard of, my enrollment in school was delayed until I was eight and one-half years old.

Fortunately my mother had taught me how to write and to do simple arithmetic. My oldest brother, George E. Redus, claims credit for teaching me to read. I think his claim is valid, for I did learn to read as he learned from his teacher. I do not recall his teaching efforts on my behalf, but I do know that the fact that he read motivated me. I suppose I sort of absorbed the reading habit from him. At any rate I was reading well at the age of three and one-half.

From 1918, when I entered school, until 1974, my life had been school-connected. The promise of freedom from rigid schedules and the opportunity to travel were enticing possibilities that retirement offered. So my last year was fraught with joyous anticipation.

I came home from school one afternoon early in January, 1974, to find some family photographs and snapshots scattered about and a few others in disarray in an old family album. When I asked Frank for an explanation, he casually remarked that my sister, Loda Belle Alton, had been searching for some old family pictures for some purpose. This evoked no curiosity on my part as Belle and I shared many common possessions.

Occasionally, Frank would ask for the address of a special friend. This was somewhat strange, for engaging in friendly correspondence certainly was not one of his major interests. Once an out-of-town friend said, "I sent a check for your affair." My reaction revealed my ignorance of the affair to which she referred, so she diplomatically changed the vein of our conversation. Numerous incidents of this and similar nature led me to suspect that something in the way of a testimonial was being planned in my honor. One day more definite information was received. I was told to keep Sunday, May 5, 1974, free, as former students and friends were planning a get-together and wanted me to be present. I was told to ask no questions and to make no efforts to learn of further details. I honored this directive. After all the years of dictating to students, it seemed only fair that they dictate to me for a change.

I thought it somewhat strange when Leona wrote from San Francisco and declared her intention to come to Texas for my birthday. I was happy at the prospect of her coming, but I did wonder why she did not wait until summer to make her visit. Since she, too, was engaged in school work, a visit in May would of necessity be of short duration. It was sometime before I associated her visit with the forthcoming get-together that had been previously mentioned to me. As time passed, by piecing together strange events and unusual remarks, I was able to learn more of the details of the plan.

On May 3, 1974, I pinned a large badge on my blouse. It read, "Thank God I Made It—65." This brought congratulations and humorous remarks from my coworkers.

About midmorning, a teacher asked me to come to the lounge immediately. I responded automatically, for I knew, as busy as I was, that no such request would be made without good reason. To my surprise and delight, I found all members of the staff and Frank assembled in the lounge. When I entered they all began to sing the traditional "Happy Birthday To You." They presented a beautifully decorated cake, and pictures were made of the happy occasion.

Later in the day an orchid corsage arrived from Helen. Throughout the day, flowers and gifts from numerous friends and parents were delivered. In the afternoon I was called to meet a bus arriving from Houston. My cup ran over as the elegant Ellen Jasper Phillips—my little Oda Ellen Jasper of Markham days—stepped off the bus and embraced me. It seemed to me that the surprises of that day would never end. Before I left school, Leona called from my home. She and Claude had flown to Dallas, rented a car, and were then enjoying Frank's barbecue in my backyard.

After school I stopped at a downtown store to make a purchase and the storekeeper said, "Mrs. Robinson, that is a beautiful news story about you in today's paper; here is a bottle of champagne with my congratulations." I thanked him and told him that I had not seen the paper. He passed me his copy, and there was my picture with a quarter page spread recounting my many years of service and announcing the public testimonial that was to be held in my honor the following Sunday.

Saturday, I received a message informing me that George and his wife Vester, and Raleigh and his wife Vivienne, would arrive in Dallas sometime that day and would be on hand for the Sunday event. I learned later that several rooms had been reserved at our town's leading hotel. Friends from Houston, San Antonio, Austin, and other points throughout the state had begun to arrive. Aside from my sisters and brothers, other relatives assembled. The James Edwards family from Columbus, Ohio, the Will Altons of Dallas, and Aunt Baby and her second husband, Earl Wright of Houston, were among the early arrivals. Uncle Pink Aycock, my mother's only living brother who then was well into his eighties, with his wife, Aunt Dolly, and some other members of their family came from Sugar Land, Texas. Mrs. Carrie Shelvin, also in her eighties and the widow of a high school teacher who had a profound influence on my life, came from Austin, a distance of almost two hundred miles.

By the time we departed from my home to the church where the testimonial was to be held, the line of cars resembled a funeral procession, but the joyous atmosphere was the exact opposite of a funeral mood. When we reached the church, I was sequestered in a small office and was told to remain there until I was formally escorted to the main auditorium. A peek proved that a capacity audience composed of a complete cross section of Palestine citizenry had assembled. I could control my emotions no longer. The tears came in torrents. My careful make-up was spoiled before I faced the audience. Any efforts to repair the damage were futile, for my tears flowed intermittently throughout the remainder of the day. When I reached my special seat that was surrounded by flowers and giant packages, I was given a copy of the program. I gasped when I saw a reproduction of a 1928 picture of myself along with a more recent one.

The theme for the occasion was "Teacher—A Many Splendored Thing." Throughout the program, my niece Karla Sue Redus played "Love Is A Many Splendored Thing." Testimonial remarks were given by former students, the school superintendent, representatives from Rusk School PTA, my church, and the local Negro Business and Professional Women's Club. In the same vein, Fuzzy (Mrs. James Edwards) and my brother Carlly spoke for the family.

By this time my lachrymal glands must have been overworked. I am sure I could have qualified as the all-time frontrunner of weeping honorees. My tears were more than tears of joy. They were tears of fulfillment. As if to add a measure of levity to the otherwise sentimental occasion, Frank presented me with a new garden hoe bedecked with a huge bow of red ribbon. The audience responded with gales of laughter when he suggested that I come down to earth and join him in his gardening enterprise. Among other presentations that followed was a book of congratulatory messages from many dignitaries including Governor Dolph Briscoe.

Then came an overwhelming surprise. Geraldyne gave a slide presentation beginning with my picture at ten months old and ending with the picture she had made a few days earlier showing me packing my belongings for my final departure from the classroom. The effect of Frank's humorous presentation was rapidly dissipating, and I was finding it increasingly difficult to control my tears. Suddenly all control was gone and tears again came in torrents, for Leona brought the second great surprise of the afternoon. On behalf of my family she presented me with a basket of forty-six red roses—"One," she said, "for each illustrative year of service."

A further surprise awaited me in the fellowship hall where refreshments were served. Huge sheet cakes bearing the words, "Congratulations DRR" had been provided through the courtesy of the Palestine Negro Business and Professional Women's Club. In the waning moments of the day's activities, I managed a smile for the press, and the most fulfilling day of my life came to an end.

The following day I broke my forty-six-year record of never taking a day off from school except in case of illness or for business reasons. I took a holiday to have a few hours with my family and to see them off on their homeward trips. Before leaving they bought all extra copies of the *Palestine Herald-Press* for Sunday, May 5, 1974, because I had been editorialized in that issue.

Later that week the Rusk school staff honored me and another coworker who also was retiring, with a dinner. My farewell gift from this highly respected group of women was a beautiful silver tray that I regard as one of my most treasured possessions.

A few days later I mailed a letter of thanks to the Palestine School Board, placed my last report on the superintendent's desk, and turned in my keys. My years of service as an elementary teacher, a homemaking teacher, a coordinator of special education, and as a principal were now history. My professional career had ended. The final curtain on that phase of my life had closed.

14

THOUGHTS AND
SECOND THOUGHTS

*T*HE PERIOD THAT I have been out of the classroom is hardly sufficient time for me to objectify my thinking about many aspects of education. For several years, however, I have had some thoughts and even some second thoughts about people and some of the institutions people have created to meet what they perceived as their needs. In recent years I have been extremely concerned about the matter in which we subvert and malign many of our institutions.

It is as though we feel that, once a social organism is created, it maintains itself and fulfills its purpose without any positive support from the members of the society it purports to serve. Many people who must be persuaded to involve themselves positively in the life of an institution will willingly and freely associate themselves with negative movements and engage in defaming tactics. This lack of awareness of, or lack of appreciation for, the role of the individual in the democratic process has influenced the changing image of the public school.

Once held in reverence as an institution of high respectability and regarded as the bulwark of American culture, our whole educational system is now under attack, and in some ways seems to be falling into disrepute. All too often and quite without justification, teachers and other school people are blamed for the plight.

Of course, schools have changed and will continue to change. If change has not been accompanied by improvement, it is largely because the change was not structured, and was not controlled by persons who were interested in improvement. It is extremely difficult for the average person to entertain the remotest notion of what a typical day at school is like for a classroom teacher. I have always thought of myself as a person of rather calm disposition, and I have tried to restrict any evidence to the contrary to my private life. But there was one remark that always infuriated me, especially when I heard it at the end of a very tiring day. The remark was, "You should not be tired. You haven't been doing anything except sitting down all day." That and similar statements represent the picture that many people have of a teacher's work day. They think of it as an eight-to-four sitting-down exercise. This is an extremely skewed conception.

I recently heard an educator say that the complete task of educating children has been placed on the teachers and, for the teacher, this is an impossible task. There is a great deal of truth in this statement. During the years I was engaged in teaching, the role of the teacher became more and more demanding. The home gradually but continuously relinquished more of its responsibilities to the school, beginning with teaching the correct method of brushing teeth in the early 1930s to supervising meals and making dental appointments in the seventies. The simple chore of supervising a lunchroom can be an arduous task when it involves encounters with normal childhood antics combined with the woeful lack of training in table manners with which so many children come to school.

Many teachers, especially those who work with lower grades, have absolutely no freedom from their charges during the whole school day. The teacher eats her lunch while supervising her pupils. During their play periods, she is supervising them. There is not even a coffee break. In some situations, classroom teachers must arrange for special supervision of their children while they visit the restroom.

For years I have protested the appalling and illogical amount of paper work that is required of classroom teachers. I know of one district in which the registration of a first-grade child entails the execution of eight separate forms, each containing much of the same information.

The time classroom teachers spend in the grading of standardized tests is inconceivable, and the logic of the practice is open to more serious question when one realizes that many such tests can be machine scored for a small fee. The practice would be somewhat less frustrating if teachers were given released time to perform the chore.

There is some justification for the negative attitude many teachers exhibit toward committee meetings and in-service activities. Most teachers will attend meetings willingly, even after hours, if they can discern some benefit. But to require teachers to work after hours in activities from which they see no meaningful results is to encourage discontent and apathy. This situation has caused many teachers to leave their professional organizations and to seek membership in labor unions.

The amount of time teachers spend in trying to improve the social skills of their pupils is incredible. The rudiments of good manners that children once received as a part of their home training must now come in large measure from the school.

These various demands make serious inroads on the teacher's time, her physical strength, and her emotional stamina, and reduces her potential to discharge satisfactorily the duties she is obligated to perform—those of teaching children. When these conditions exist, either singly or in combination, to such an extent that they threaten a teacher's confidence and courage, even an experienced, dedicated teacher may yield to frustration.

Certainly all failures of the schools are not the result of external forces. Part of the responsibility must be borne by the teachers themselves. I have often privately questioned the positive value of the teachers' lounge, but the lounge, like all other man-made contrivances, yields to the will of man. Whether it proves to be a liability or an asset is determined by the quality of the judgment of those who use it. The terms "lounge lady" and "lounge sitter" are not always misnomers. Many tax dollars are wasted while teachers sip coffee in the lounge, or visit in the hallways while their pupils throw the traditional spitballs or otherwise engage in undisciplined and meaningless behavior.

A creative teacher is indispensable to creative teaching, and it is a sad but true commentary that too many teachers enter the profession without recognizing this basic fact. Equally disturbing is

the fact that too many principals, supervisors, and people in supportive roles are unable to provide teachers with the needed help.
The result is a slavish dependence on guide books, commercial pack-
ets, and mechanical gadgetry. Each of these has its place and each,
used in connection with sound judgment, has contributed im-
measurably to successful teaching. But it is a gross error to rely on
teaching aids to fulfill the role of a teacher.

The early 1960s saw a colossal expenditure of money for hardware, because there were those in decision making positions who
mistakingly equated the acquisition of teaching aids with quality
education. There can be found in storerooms in school buildings
throughout this country thousands of dollars worth of dusty teaching machines, many of which have seen little use and some of which
have seen none. These machines are perfectly reliable teaching devices, and they were purchased in good faith, but they have contributed little to student achievement. Many teachers do not know
how to use the machines; others are uncomfortable with them and
still others resent the fact that they had no share in the selection.

Another factor that has affected the quality of education negatively, especially in recent years, is the myth that drastically different teaching techniques are necessary for teaching children of
different ethnic groups. The responsibility of teachers is to teach
children and not ethnicity. The basic needs of children are the
same. In the process of meeting these basic needs, special needs will
surface. They may be physical, emotional, mental, or cultural.
Whatever the nature, they should be dealt with, and this will of
course require special techniques. The error is in making incorrect
prejudgments based on the assumption that all children of a certain
ethnic group are alike, and that they differ markedly from all other
children in another ethnic group. This erroneous belief sometimes
causes teachers to doubt their capability to teach across ethnic lines,
and it also results in stereotyping in the counseling regime.

The decree to desegregate public schools produced the greatest
social trauma the South has known since the Emancipation Procla-
mation. Few indeed are the people who escaped its impact. Both
white and minority groups suffered, but in different ways. Many

whites felt that it was demeaning to have to share their schools with a group who had heretofore been consigned to a role of subservience. For the same reason many objected to sharing public dining rooms and hotels with minority groups. Both groups suffered, but my thought is that blacks suffered more, for, in addition to the emotional trauma, many suffered the threat or the reality of economic reprisal.

Some districts simply and forthrightly dismissed all of their black teachers without giving a reason. Others used superficial reasons to gain their diabolic end. Black principals were shamefully demoted to menial jobs, but were given impressive titles. Many drove buses while wearing the title, assistant superintendent or executive assistant.

The hiring of blacks in some districts reached a dead standstill. When HEW or some other checking agency made inquiry regarding the practice, the explanation was given that qualified blacks could not be found or that no blacks had applied. An examination of the files would reveal an absence of applications from black teachers. Some districts had practiced this ruse for several years before it was learned that the files remained void of applications from black teachers because all such applications were returned to the sender or consigned to the wastebasket.

The position of blacks was not always accurately reported to the state agency. The Texas Public School Directory sometimes listed a black person as holding a certain position, when in reality, his performance was in no way identified with the job title.

The number of advanced degrees held by blacks is still a matter of amazement to many whites. Some superintendents tended to discount the quality of the advanced degrees held by black teachers, because most were earned at predominantly black institutions.

In the late 1940s and early fifties, many black teachers who earned the master's degree never reported the fact to their school officials. In most instances, this meant a loss in salary because the master's degree automatically moved one into a higher pay bracket. A black man in the academic procession marching to receive his master's degree said to a friend, "I am going to get this piece of paper, but I am going to put it in the bottom of my trunk, for my superintendent does not have a master's degree, and if he finds out that I have one, he will surely fire me."

One school board met a shocking surprise when, in trying to cope with desegregation, it voted to give priority in hiring to those teachers holding advanced degrees. The surprise came when the files revealed that more blacks than whites held the favored credentials.

If the black teacher has suffered, it stands to reason that the black student has suffered more. The number of black students who graduate with honors from integrated high schools is exceedingly small, and little is being done to reverse the trend. Sheer numerical ratio would indicate that in a normal grouping, more whites than blacks would receive the honors, but questions arise in districts where a black never receives the honor. Many people feel, and with considerable support, that, except in athletics, blacks are given little encouragement, and in some instances, measures are taken to assure low grades. Many black students with excellent scholastic ratings through junior high watch in horror as their possibilities of graduating from high school with honors disappear. As if by design, low grades creep intermittently into their records—a low grade in literature this reporting period and a low grade in mathematics the next time. It is strongly suspected that the pattern is too precise to be accidental or the grades valid.

Too much has militated against the black student. He lost his principal and in many instances his teacher also. He was denied the recognition that achievement brings except on the athletic field, and sometimes even there. His trophies were no longer on display to inspire him. His punishments were liable to be more frequent and more severe than those imposed on his white counterparts. Even the name of his school was changed. If a school's name honored a black hero such as Martin Luther King, George Washington Carver, or Emmett Scott, it was liable to be changed to such designation as Eastside School or Northside Middle School. An interesting example of name change occurred when a former black school named Booker T. Washington suddenly became George Washington. Little wonder then that the dropout rate among blacks is cause for national concern.

Considering the years of rigid segregation with separate drinking fountains, separate dining rooms, separate toilet facilities, separate traveling arrangements, and disfranchisement at the polls, it borders on the miraculous that desegregation proceeded as smoothy as it did. Very few communities in Texas took concrete steps to prepare for the change, and the state provided very little leadership in this regard. Until the late 1960s, my own district held separate administrators' meetings for black and white principals and separate staff meetings for black and white teachers.

While making a campaign speech in the Butler community in Freestone County, Governor Allan Shivers stood on the bed of Frank's truck and discouraged the desegregation of schools. He accurately predicted the wholesale dismissal of black teachers that would accompany the desegregation effort. His grasp of the situation was remarkable, but evidently the idea of using his executive power to develop and implement effective orientation strategies never entered his mind. If he did perceive of such action as being the responsibility of his office, he may have thought it politically unfeasible to initiate it.

It was more than a decade after the 1954 Supreme Court decision when Texas made serious efforts to comply with the ruling. During the intervening years, apprehension grew, fears crystallized, several administrators suffered fatal heart attacks, and in my town a white lady opined to her black maid, "Now you know it would not be right for your son and my granddaughter to sit together at school." The maid asked how and why it would be wrong since the two of them had sat together for years. The employer's weak reply was simply, "That's different." Then she wished to be dead before such a wild and dangerous possibility became a reality. Her wish was granted.

In actuality, physical desegregation of most schools in Texas occurred without any spiritual or emotional desegregation and certainly without any integration. Even after schools were desegregated and desensitizing workshops were provided on the state level, many local districts did not choose to participate. Some superintendents and principals refused to announce the schedule of such meetings, thus many teachers who might have benefited from participation did not even know that the meetings were being held. One superintendent told me frankly that he considered such meetings a waste of time.

Often when a black teacher was sent to a predominately white school, or vice versa, the announcement was not made until the last minute. I know of one case in which a black teacher was given three days to transfer from the all-black school, where she had worked for several years, to a school that was predominately white. There was another case where the superintendent walked into a white teacher's room and directed her to remove all of her personal belongings at the end of the day, and report on the morrow to an all-black school.

This kind of abrupt and traumatic change creates a need for special human-relation skills. Professional training as such is not sufficient to fortify most teachers against the strangeness of their new environment. Fortunate indeed was the teacher, white or black, who brought no chip on her shoulder; who could hear denigrating terms without feeling shame, or resorting to retaliation; who possessed no shock level and a ready sense of humor. The teacher working with small children probably needed these attributes even more than those working with upper grades. The dictates of society provided some veneer for older students, but primary youngsters often spoke and acted with the stark innocence that characterizes the very young.

An interesting example of this occurred in my classroom at a time when my second grade pupils were drawing Halloween characters. Our plan was to complete our drawings and then share them as a group experience. One little blond, gray-eyed, seven-year-old completed his drawing and was so overcome with impatience he could not wait for the sharing period. He rushed up, placed his arms lovingly about my waist, looked directly into my face, and asked in all innocence, "Mrs. Robinson, do you know what I drew?" I said, "No baby, what did you draw?" With equal innocence, yet with the joy of accomplishment ringing in his voice, he said, "I drew two niggers, and I gave them some long ears." I could not destroy that child's moment of ecstasy. I could not fail to share the joy of his accomplishment. To him, he had simply drawn two Halloween characters, and in his guilelessness, he did not identify me and probably any of his several black classmates with the picture he had drawn. It was several days later that we discussed such terms as nigger, cracker, redneck, pepper-belly, and greaser, and tried to arrive at some decision as to whether or not these were pleasant and friendly terms to use.

One day two of my white second-grade boys rushed up to me. As their words spilled forth in unison, it became clear that my ancestry was under discussion, and they had come to have the argument settled. Finally the voice of the more forward one gained ascendency, and he asked, "Mrs. Robinson, aren't you half-white?" Although genetically I probably could have answered truthfully in the affirmative, I saw no point in maximizing the ethnic factor. Moreover, a white coworker, with whom I was conversing, had turned an uncomfortable rosy red, so I said, "My dear, we are all so mixed up, who knows? Let us all try to be good citizens, whatever we are racially. Now run along to lunch." The boys left apparently satisfied, but my coworker had difficulty in regaining her composure and very soon found reason to terminate the conversation. I believed then as I do now that that child's question grew out of some adult discussion that he had been exposed to.

I sincerely believe that for young children, a teacher, especially if they like her, is colorless. A group of white youngsters rushed to a black teacher one day reporting in a chorus, "Mrs. Jones, the niggers are out there beating up Sam." Without batting the figurative eye, the wise teacher said, "Thank you. I'm coming right out and stop the niggers from beating up Sam."

If it were possible for these young Americans to reach maturity with the same color blindness they possess as children, the dream of a democratic society just might be realized. But this is not yet to be. There were those, and I was among them, who felt in the early days of desegregation that the children would make integration a reality, but we failed to recognize the impact of home influence. It is the home in most communities that keeps racism alive, and both races are guilty. Black parents pass their mistrust of whites on to their children, and white parents transmit their racial prejudices on to their children. Together they continue to pick the sore, forgetting or not caring about the truth of the old proverb which states, a sore that is picked cannot heal. Together they create an environment suitable for the perpetuation of racism. Often the efforts of the young to overcome racial barriers are met with parental rebuff.

A black youngster, on seeing his white teacher on a downtown street, greeted her with a cheerful voice and a smiling face. His mother asked, "Why are you speaking to that old white woman?" The boy's reply was, "She's no old white woman, she's my teacher." The mother, set in the concrete of her bias, retorted, "She's still an old white woman to me." In the same vein, a white junior-high student accompanying her mother in a supermarket attempted to wave at her black teacher across the aisle. The mother struck her daughter's hand down, and the young lady suffered obvious embarrassment. If parents could only realize the tragic consequences of exposing their children to such experiences, they would rethink their own philosophy and perhaps change their tactics.

I have been pained on numerous occasions to see the inner struggle and ambivalence of some of my white students when they found it necessary to greet me in the presence of their parents. Young children who usually met me at school with embraces and an unrestricted display of affection became different persons when the type of greeting they could extend to their teacher was determined by parental sanction. I shall always remember the look of bafflement and frustration on the faces of some of those lovable children as they sought unsuccessfully to understand why a teacher who loved them and whom they loved at school, away from their parents, became something of a pariah when she was met on the street in the parents' presence.

Because I have considerable contact with multiracial groups, and because I have many friends among white and brown people as well as blacks, I am frequently asked to assess the status of race relations in this country. People wonder what I perceive as the strengths and weaknesses of our efforts to bring about integration, and they wonder if I have any suggestions for strengthening our efforts. A pointed question that I hear with great frequency is, "Are blacks better off since the desegregation of schools?"

Since the whole spectrum of race relations is in its simplest form a matter of human relations, it is impossible to measure its status or progress with mathematical precision, for human nature is not always predictable and every individual is different, and so is every situation involving human beings. When I think of race relations, I do not limit myself to schools, or to housing, or to public accommodations, or to transportation. I see, or at least I try to see, the whole spectrum. I use the civil rights legislation of the mid-sixties as the pivot and compare what has transpired since with what existed before. I think every group in America is better off since the passage of those laws. Blacks, of course, enjoy more comfortable accommodations, and their doing so has in no way affected the well-being of whites. The money spent by blacks in areas once denied them has helped to boost the nation's economy. In recent years, studies have shown that the amount of money spent by blacks in this country is a sum worthy of economic consideration. Some social scientists feel that economics and not morality provided the basis for the whole civil rights movement.

Whatever the cause, I would have to be totally insensitive to the past not to feel that conditions are better now. I remember all too well the Jim Crow cars and the separate waiting rooms at the railroad stations. My parents were always careful to arrive at the station with time to spare so there would be time to purchase our tickets without fret and anxiety. The agent in small towns generally had to serve two windows located on opposite sides of his office. He rarely sold the tickets on a first-come, first-served basis. The white passengers usually were served first, and this sometimes meant last-minute frustrations for the blacks, or colored, as the railroad designation read.

As late as 1952, while en route from San Francisco to Houston to attend my father's funeral, my sister and I were asked at the Texas border to move to a segregated car. We refused on the grounds that we were interstate passengers whose trip originated in a non-Jim Crow state. Having no legal power to force us to move, the conductor engaged in behavior that evidently was intended to embarrass us. He stalked down the aisle several times loudly proclaiming that the farther we moved into Texas, " . . . the worse things will get." Each time I replied quietly but firmly, "That's a chance we'll take."

I never enter a hotel room without remembering the tired feet of Rosa Parks, the black woman who refused to relinquish her seat on a segregated bus, and the ensuing struggles that changed things for black people. I can appreciate the change all the more, for I still remember in the early 1950s, while returning from Mexico City, we planned our schedule so as to be in Mexico at nightfall, for in that foreign country, we could secure comfortable lodging. That night, and many times thereafter, Frank and I have relived the stark injustice that we knew on that occasion. Like our parents, we were natives of Texas. Our grandparents had been slaves in Texas. We were schooled in Texas and we worked and paid taxes in the state. We had money to pay for the desired accommodations, but the laws of our state denied us this simple human comfort only because our skins were black.

Were it not for the indignities imposed by Jim Crow laws, many of the provisions would be ludicrous. Once while driving from Palestine to Shreveport, Louisiana, I stopped at a small town some fifty miles from Palestine to have my car serviced. I waited until the attendant had begun to supply the gasoline and was checking under the hood before I stepped into the ladies room. The attendant opened the door that was not fitted with a lock and said rather caustically, "You can't use that." Without changing my position and without any effort to recoup my feminine modesty, I replied, "I'm sorry, sir, but I am already in the process of using it."

Surely the stupidity of the extreme separatism under which we lived for so many years was apparent to anyone who chose to analyze the situation sanely. With the innocence of a young child, yet with the wisdom of a sage, my young nephew once asked the pivotal question, "Why can't I drink at that fountain?" Yes, why? When we as a nation began to ask why, we began to find some sound practical answers.

The way men treat each other can be affected by legislation, but the way they feel about each other cannot be legislated. Feelings change either positively or negatively as knowledge increases, and knowledge increases through association and honest communication. A white teacher recently reported with happy surprise, his discovery that "Niggers don't stink anymore." I do not think he realizes yet that all blacks were never guilty of body odor just as all whites were never guilty. He is unaware of this fact because of his prior limited contact with blacks.

At best, integrated situations in school are contrived, and contrived situations are not as conducive to the development of amicable relationships as natural situations are. Therefore, I think if true integration is ever to be realized in America, it will grow from desegregated housing and not from desegregated schools. There is a naturalness in a relationship that springs from mutual need. When kids play together in the backyard, when housewives exchange recipes and share coffee breaks, and fathers pool rides, America will have reached the embryonic stage in integration that promises a new birth of freedom.

The passage of civil rights legislation is not an end within itself. There are positive approaches that all citizens need to take to insure its effective implementation. As a group, black people should strive to overcome their feelings of vindictiveness. I receive strong protests sometimes when I remind blacks that there is not a white person alive who held any of our ancestors in slavery. Consequently we are not justified in holding any contemporary white responsible for our previous condition of servitude. This further means that we are not justified in directing any vindictive measures toward a generation that is of itself guiltless.

I receive equally strong protests when I tell white groups that they should cease to penalize the blacks for becoming what the whites have made them. Barriers have been placed in the black man's way. Opportunities have been withheld from him, and there is scarcely a black person in America today who has not been victimized to some extent by these practices. Like Edwin Markham's "Man With The Hoe," the blacks in America have been betrayed, plundered, profaned, and disinherited. He is no longer the thing the Lord God made because he has been molded by another craftsman who fashioned him for subservient purposes.

Black people should divest themselves of the belief that being

black makes one beautiful or makes one eligible for special conces-
sions. They need to realize that the primary purpose for hiring a
worker is to have that worker contribute to the economy in the
production of goods or in the provision of services. Therefore, it
is a skill and not a black face that should be brought to the labor
market.

On the other hand, employers—most of whom are white—should
execute justice in their hiring practices. Many impressive applications find their way to the wastebasket simply because the applicant is black. Employers are often unwilling to provide the same
type of on-the-job training for blacks that they provide for their
white employees. If the first experience in hiring a black does not
prove satisfactory, many employers are reluctant to hire another,
but they would not dream of refusing to hire whites because of an
earlier failure. Some employers are reluctant to hire blacks because
they feel that whites will not work with them. Some refuse to pro-
mote blacks because they fear that whites will not accept supervision from blacks. Each of these assumptions is based on a myth,
and is being disproved in numerous ways and on various levels
throughout the country.

Extreme sensitivity on the part of blacks, while understandable,
works to their detriment. Our country is now pioneering in the
area of human rights, and pioneer life is always rugged. It is fraught
with handicaps and discomforts. We are human, and we are weak.
Even when we strive to be our best selves, we sometimes err. We
make statements and comments that are entirely innocent in intent, but may very well be painful to others. In describing my bargaining techniques in Africa, I used the expression, "jewing the sel-
ler down," meaning that I had successfully contended for a lower
price than that originally asked. How embarrassed I was when I
remembered that I had a Jewish friend in the group, and how happy
I was that she was a woman of deep human understanding with a
forgiving heart.

A councilman in one of Texas's larger cities recently found it
necessary to apologize for using the old expression, "There's a
nigger in the woodpile." In his apology, he explained that no racial
insult was meant. Regardless of the innocence of his intent, his

words had greatly incensed some of his constituents.

Once I took my class on a field trip. The guide who conducted us through the plant seemed compelled to direct his remarks to my aide, who was white. She continued to remind him that I was the teacher and that I was in charge. It made not one whit of difference in his procedure. He was absolutely incapable, at that moment, of regarding me as the person in charge, as there was a white woman along. I recognized his grave inadequacy and forgave him even while he continued his violation of protocol.

In 1974 I served on a national committee, the members of which were from different parts of the United States, and most were strangers to each other. My only contact with the chairman had been by letter. When I opened the door of my hotel room in response to his knock, his gulp of surprise was so audible he was embarrassed. Throughout our meeting together, he made overt efforts to redeem himself, and I graciously accepted his efforts. His shock was understandable if not reasonable. It had never entered his mind that since I was human there was at least a possibility that I might be a black human being or a brown one. He only thought white.

These experiences give some index of the constraints imposed upon the minds of many white people and the narrow purview of their thinking. It represents a type of perceptual enslavement. I have a friend who frequently says that the white people of America are bound by a system of social slavery that is as restrictive as the physical slavery the blacks once knew. I find it difficult to disagree with him. When whites free themselves from the social fetters that dictate their actions, they will be at liberty to choose their friends on the basis of individual worth and common interests, and they will be as comfortable associating with blacks in public as they are in private.

It appears to me that the issues people are most inclined to talk to me about are related to education, race relations, and life in the United States as compared to life in other countries. They seem to have the erroneous idea that because I have traveled in forty-five of the fifty states of the Union and in many foreign countries, I have acquired a mass of knowledge about other countries and therefore must be in position to make a valid and comprehensive analysis of different forms of government and should hold a key to "the good life." I suppose being biased in favor of one's own country is common among most human beings. So I admit my inability to objectively compare lifestyles in other countires with that in the United States. Having grown up in an era when patriotism was woven into a child's training like yarn into a fabric, my pro-American feelings are probably nurtured as much by sentimentality as by the actual merit of the American way.

Since my visits to foreign countries have all been of short duration, my observations have been cursory at best. Wherever I have gone, I have found some things to admire in the lifestyle of the people, and I have found some things that were distasteful to me, but that is exactly how I feel about the way of life in America.

I have only to recall the school I visited in Nepal where the students, composed of the privileged few, were eager to learn, yet hampered by a total lack of instructional materials, and unable to realize the benefits of our system of free education. When I think further of the children I saw in Peru who have never seen, and probably never will see in a lifetime, a written word, I think the impossible task of educating all of America's children is still a worthy effort. When I remember the stolid, abject hopelessness in the eyes and movements of children in India and the same in Niger and Mali in West Africa, I say to myself that this could never happen in a functioning democracy. For democracy demands of its adherents responsibility and self-discipline and, without a knowledge of himself and his world, man is not responsible and cannot discipline himself.

I feel that in most foreign countries I have visited, the people have more reverence for tradition than we have. They appreciate simple things and noncommercial experiences more than Americans do, and I am inclined to think of this as a meritorious trait. With prideful voice the guide describes the age of a building in terms of centuries to a group of awe-struck, gawking American tourists who have spent a small fortune to leave an American city where fine historic buildings just a few decades old yield to the onslaught of a demolition squad to "make way for progress." American's appreciation of simple joys and beauties seems to be on the wane. We have become too "things" oriented. Consequently too many people have too many things, and many of the things have been acquired too easily.

The maintenance of a welfare system for those who need it is a laudable practice in any country, but there is something abominable about a system that creates an ever-increasing number of needy people and perpetuates their needy state through exploitation and deprivation. America is a land of "enough." Everyone in this country should be permitted to procure his share of what America has to offer, and he should be expected to work toward the procurement of that share. This would improve the American work ethic and provide millions with a joy they have never known—the joy of earning. It is the worker who produces and earns and helps maintain our democracy as it was conceived, and not the needy recipient of the welfare check.

Surely America has its weaknesses, some of which are shocking and frightening. Surely there are problems that seem to defy solution. Surely we have never become the melting pot that was once considered a worthy goal. Surely America is not yet the land of the free, but there is built into its governmental structure a base upon which men can stand and fight for the freedom that is constitutionally theirs. There is built into the structure mechanisms for rectifying wrongs, for protecting the selfhood, and for providing every citizen with the opportunity of becoming a person of worth. In my thinking, these are the basic factors that primarily distinguish America from any other country I have visited and these are the features of our government that cause me to prefer to live in America.

The democratic concept is the most alluring and perhaps the most impossible dream man has ever entertained, and to share in that dream is a blessing that one recognizes more as he visits foreign lands. The more exposure an American has to foreign cultures and lifestyles, the more he is likely to appreciate America as it really exists with its faults and with its glories. I know that this has been my personal experience. The same feeling has been expressed by my nephew, Colonel Carlly Lee Alton (Joe to the family), a career military man who has spent many years in foreign countries. Recently Joe wrote: "I have always been proud of being an American; recently I have begun to think of myself as being downright blessed because I am an American."

Joe spoke my sentiments. My blessings have been legionary. I do indeed consider myself blessed to be an American. I consider myself blessed to have lived and worked in America during a period of dramatic social, economic, educational, and cultural change. I know I am blessed to have had for my parents Caleb and Susie Redus, who inspired me to enter the teaching profession and who sacrificed to that end.

Whether the school day ended at three, three-thirty, or four o'clock, I was blessed with the privilege to ring the bell.